A LEAP INTO THE UNKNOWN

Marie Sumner

Book Guild Publishing
Sussex, England

First published in Great Britain in 2012 by
The Book Guild Ltd
Pavilion View
19 New Road
Brighton, BN1 1UF

Copyright © Marie Sumner 2012

The right of Marie Sumner to be identified as the author of
this work has been asserted by her in accordance with the
Copyright, Designs and Patents Act 1988.

All rights reserved. No part of this publication may be reproduced,
transmitted, or stored in a retrieval system, in any form or by any means,
without permission in writing from the publisher, nor be otherwise circulated
in any form of binding or cover other than that in which it is published and
without a similar condition being imposed on the subsequent purchaser.

Typesetting in Garamond by
Ellipsis Digital Limited, Glasgow

Printed and bound in Great Britain by
CPI Group (UK) Ltd, Croydon, CR0 4YY

A catalogue record for this book is available from The British Library.

ISBN 978 1 84624 791 0

A LEAP INTO THE UNKNOWN

1

Here I am; a stylish, senior, English lady, sitting all alone in an elegant house, surrounded by a beautifully cultivated garden in the awe-inspiring country of New Zealand.

I often marvel at the journey I have experienced getting here. Back home in England, I was a retired schoolteacher married to a doctor, and consequently was leading a very busy life in the community. I was also a successful after-dinner speaker, talking about the origins of the British music hall together with some background social history, while throwing in a few songs for good measure. Yes – I was 'somebody' then, but now, in comparison, I am 'nobody'. I have completely lost my identity. You may be wondering how such a drastic change could occur in my life. How someone who was at the hub of social activity could be so out on a limb. It all happened when my dear husband Colin passed away.

Of course, we all know how the loss of a loved one can change lives, but do we really understand the utter pain, despair and confusion it brings until we are actually experiencing it for ourselves? I think not. I certainly had no idea how painful it could be until it happened to me. Although surrounded by a network of good friends that we had known for years and who were giving me all the support humanly possible, the huge empty space in my life was impossible to fill and nothing seemed to bring me the slightest comfort. When someone kindly assured me that I was still young enough to find another partner, I realised that only I knew and understood the exact intensity of the pain I was experiencing and, although they were trying to be kind, I wondered how they could be so insensitive.

I was disorientated and shocked and yet I seemed to have a cool acceptance that I had things to do. In the past, I had always tried to control events in my life, to orchestrate happenings, and now I had to accept that fate had taken a hand in the design of things to come. My life had changed in an instant and I knew that I simply had to go with the flow in order to survive.

As a result of this trauma, one of the first things to happen was that I lost two stone in weight. That was a nice surprise. After years of dieting, sensible eating, buying flowing garments to hide the little lumps and bumps etc. here I was with my heart's desire, a figure as thin as a pin. I must say that at least brought me a glimmer of pleasure! My bottom and tummy had simply melted away and with the crutch of my trousers hanging somewhere in the region of my knees, I looked like Yogi Bear. Naturally, all my friends said I ought to eat more to build my strength but I just couldn't. I knew I didn't have to wobble around with that extra two stone in order to operate efficiently. I could hardly wait to do what I am sure most ladies would do – hit the shops! Even in my traumatised state, I knew where to head! I don't think I have ever bought so many clothes in such a short space of time and, in spite of my great sadness, at least I felt physically wonderful. In fact, when admiring myself in the mirror, I actually thought 'Good gracious, if I were a member of the opposite sex – I'd fancy you!' Call me fickle, but I felt truly comforted when sliding into my new clothes each morning without that awful palaver of lying on the bed in order to flatten my tummy, thus enabling the zip to connect. I had lost little pockets of fat all over, right down to my feet; even they were sliding into my shoes more comfortably. I think I had experienced 'melt down'. Yes, physically I felt good and resolved I would never be a plump little granny again. I recall reading somewhere that you must pay attention to your clothes and appearance because if you feel good on the outside, it will help you feel good on the inside and I must admit that it took very little effort for me to do just that!

Does death give advance warning, I wonder? On reflection, I realised that my husband had been slowing down quite considerably over the last few years. In fact he used to say that he was in God's departure lounge and yet it didn't really register with me at the time. Being an educated and wise man, he would make all sorts of interesting comments about life in general and I became used to it, even letting it occasionally float over my head. We all know how the familiarity of a long-standing relationship can sometimes induce a trance-like state. But now I started to ponder on things he had said and wondered if he was gently trying to warn me that the end was near. After all, being a medical man, he must have realised it himself. Of course, if this was the case, I now feel utterly dreadful. One of my real regrets is that I feel I let him down at a time when I should have been more attentive, listening to him and comforting him.

They say there are several stages that one has to pass through with bereavement. One is guilt – I'm very relieved to say that I feel no guilt because I'm sure I always tried to do the best as I knew it, but my great sadness really is a sense of regret. In fact, to pass a day without regret must surely be a great achievement in life and now I have learned to try and live in a way that would cause no regrets to surface.

Of course, all the official stuff had to be dealt with and the first thing was to register his death. I'll never forget emerging from the registrar's office with the death certificate in my hand. It seemed as though I held his life there and had actually finalised his existence.

As the weeks drifted by, there was very little change. Although looking stunning on the outside, I was continually weeping inside, I just couldn't seem to stop the steady flow and even when driving, found myself with tears spilling down my cheeks. The words of a familiar song summed up my feelings so well:

> The sun is out, the sky is blue. There's not a cloud to spoil the view, but it's raining, raining in my heart. The weather man says clear today, he doesn't know you've gone away and it's raining, raining in my heart. Oh misery, misery. What's going to become of me. I tell the blues they mustn't show, but soon these tears are bound to flow, 'cos it's raining, raining in my heart.
>
> (Felice and Boudleaux Bryant.)

I was getting totally exasperated with myself. Not only was I grieving for Colin, I realised that I was grieving for myself too. I was falling into a terribly depressed state. I dread to think what my friends must have been feeling about me.

Just two months later, a further bombshell was dropped. My youngest daughter Sue, who lived near me with her family, came to tell me that they planned to emigrate to New Zealand. Her husband had been offered a job and they were all set to go. I could see immediately that it would be a good move for them and their three young sons, and of course tried to show my enthusiasm, but I had already lost my eldest daughter Jan to New Zealand and was instantly overwhelmed with the idea of them being on the other side of the world. I would very rarely see them and thus be absolutely all alone.

I think the sorrow I felt for my husband then turned into a greater sorrow for myself and all that was happening to me. Everything that was stable in my life seemed now to be hurtling out of control. What would be the purpose in my life now? Who would be there for me? What would I do? I knew I was feeling very confused and decided the best thing for me to do was to stay indoors until the fog cleared, and, I must say, it was a very frightening experience. Nevertheless, I knew I would get through it. I had to – other people had, so I resolved I would too.

One of my hobbies is to collect profound and interesting quotes and in the depths of my despair, I went to my books to seek some sort of comfort and help and found the following:

Claire Rayner had simply said; 'This too will pass.'

A LEAP INTO THE UNKNOWN

'Experience is not what happens to you. It is what you do with what happens to you.' (Aldous Huxley.)

'True courage consists not in flying from the storms of life but in braving and steering through them with prudence . . .' (Hannah Webster Foster.)

And from an author unknown to me; 'Life ain't all ya want but it's all ya got so accept it. Stick a geranium in your hat and be happy.' I particularly liked that one. It seemed so down to earth, full of fun and yet very wise.

Still fishing for help in coming to terms with my predicament, I thought of the two masks of the theatre – tragedy and comedy – and how they depicted what life is really about. I also thought about the mythical phoenix, fabled to have risen from its own ashes, and many other inspirational ideas about life. 'Yes, I can do it!' I thought, 'especially now I am so delighted with my new svelte figure. At least I look a million dollars!' I was swanning around, totally unaware that the option for more mature ladies seems to be either a plump figure and a pleasing face, or a slim figure and a face that hangs like curtains. It's rather like the option one faces when choosing rose bushes for the garden. You either go for perfume or magnificent blooms. It seems that you can't have both. My friends told me much later, when I was strong enough to take it, that although I had the slim, shapely figure of a young woman, I had lost my sparkle and my face was looking sadly haggard. This, of course, only added to my despair.

There had been an occasion when it was brought home to me how silly I was, clutching at straws of delight in this superficial way. While I was in a shopping centre, I noticed a very stylish, shapely lady of rather advanced years walking past. She was very nicely turned out and it was obvious that she was full of confidence and feeling rather pleased with her looks. I felt pleased for her too but I couldn't help thinking, 'Silly old bat, she can't hide her age!' How spiteful is that? As it happened, I passed her a couple of times more and then it hit me. I had been glimpsing my own reflection in the shop windows! The silly old bat was actually me! I was both horrified and amused – but thanked God that my sense of humour extends to laughing at myself.

Never mind, the fog seemed to be clearing a little and I was beginning to feel that perhaps I could carry on by myself.

Colin and I had always loved the house and area in which we lived and I saw no reason to downsize now I was alone. As I looked around, I could see how sadly shabby and lived in it had become and I thought a 'face lift' would be good for both of us. It would also give me an exciting project to fill my thoughts. The first thing I did was to trawl through all the notices and bits of paper that seemed to have accumulated around the telephone in the kitchen. Oh dear, that caused another rollercoaster ride of emotion. Notes from me to him; his handwritten notes to me; notes and invitations from friends – all reminding me of the busy life we had led and how every day seemed so empty now. It was just as the tears started to spill again that I came upon a message from him to me written in bold felt tip pen. It simply said 'Press on Marie'. We had been sent details of how to update the channels on our TV. He had obviously studied them and written down his opinion for me, but I now saw this as a real message of encouragement. I clasped it to my breast, hugged it and kissed it and thanked him for sending it to me. Oh, have I mentioned before that I continually talk to him? My only comfort is knowing that his spirit is still living and with me. It certainly seemed a real coincidence to come face to face with such a boldly written note from him saying just the sort of encouraging thing he used to say and at a time when I needed it most. I took the message, trimmed round the edges and ran it through the laminating machine. I have that message stuck in a prominent place in my kitchen to this very day and often look at it to remind myself – when I'm feeling low – to simply 'press on'.

Having had a thorough spring clean and sorted out all the surface clutter that accumulates, I set about repainting all the rooms. Well, actually, I didn't do the painting myself, I got two professional painters and decorators in to do the job.

One thing that's quite odd about getting old is that you still have the confidence and enthusiasm to tackle the jobs you used to do and yet, when you try to mount the stepladders and feel the wobble, you know you just have limitations that have suddenly crept up on you totally unawares. I can remember being so keen at one time that I used to get up at the crack of dawn, bursting with energy. On one occasion I had done about two hours work before my husband even surfaced. He walked wearily into the kitchen to be confronted with a totally naked lady up a ladder, wearing only a handkerchief on her head, tied in the customary fashion that elderly English gentlemen adopt when visiting the seaside. Once he recovered from the shock and I explained that it had seemed the obvious thing to do, saving splashes on my clothes and planning a good soak in the bath when I had finished the job, he could see the sense of it. We had a good laugh, but he made me promise never to do any exterior decorating. I find old memories like these constantly slip into my mind.

I must tell you about the decorators. They were a father and son team and that impressed me immediately. They were both good-looking men who really seemed to be interested in the work that they were doing. So far, so good. I told them what I wanted and from that time on, had absolutely great faith in them. Not only were they father and son but also the best of friends. Add the fact that they were also good and honest tradesmen and I felt very well satisfied. I soon become addicted to listening to their general chit-chat. They thoroughly enjoyed each other's company and would chatter away in the manner one would generally associate with a mother and daughter. It was so addictive, I just couldn't stop myself from eavesdropping and I spent many an interesting hour listening to the two of them.

It was not long before I was living in a completely redecorated house, with a wardrobe full of wonderfully stylish clothes (designed for stick pins, I might add) and had all the freedom in the world to be myself – to eat when I wanted to, to drink as much as I wanted, to read and to listen to music when I wanted, to even have complete charge of the television controls and to go to bed when I wanted to. So you might wonder what more could I possibly want in life, but without purpose the days – as such days always do – ended in disintegration.

My friends were overwhelmingly kind to me, taking me out and about, but I still had to unlock that door and go in every night to absolutely nothing. I had tried to be brave and to accept the fact that Sue and her family would be much better off in New Zealand but I just couldn't face the fact that, in spite of all I had around me, I would be totally alone. There seemed to be no other alternative but to follow them to New Zealand, to be near them and also to be reunited with my other daughter, Jan. To have the whole family nearby. I certainly didn't want to be a burden, but I was their mother and it seemed only natural that I would want to be near my loved ones.

I remember when Jan first moved to NZ, the beautiful singer Hayley Westenra had made a CD of Maori Songs and I used to play them constantly. I thought it would bring her nearer to me, but actually it nearly always caused me to weep. Why do we beat ourselves up so much? It's like having the remaining scab from an injury and continually picking it, not giving it chance to heal at all and actually causing the healing process to take longer than it should.

I felt very apprehensive in leaving all that I had known and loved to commit myself to a totally different existence, but my girls were my flesh and blood – my family – and they were all on the other side of the world, as far away as they could possibly be. Yes, I just had to go, to be near them. Of course, I've always known that they had their lives to live but I knew that I had enough behind me, both in character and in finance, to operate by myself without being a problem to anyone, and yet I felt I would have a safety net there to catch and comfort me whenever I fell, if ever I did. It all became quite clear to me; I would emigrate to New Zealand.

Funnily enough, I had just read the quote, 'An optimist sees an opportunity in every calamity; a pessimist sees a calamity in every opportunity'. (Winton Churchill.) I was determined to see that the whole upshot of my recent traumas was to be an opportunity to start a new life – a life I didn't particularly feel enthusiastic about and wasn't prepared for. What else could I do but go with the flow?

I contacted several estate agents with a view to putting the house on the market and I applied to New Zealand House for a Resident's Visa. How about that for being assertive? I simply amazed myself! As Agnes De Mille said; 'No trumpets sound when important decisions of our life are made. Destiny is made known silently.'

'Acceptance is not submission; it is the acknowledgement of the facts of a situation. Then deciding what you're going to do about it.' (Kathleen Casey Theisen.)

I can't say that selling the house was a traumatic experience because, thankfully, everyone that came to view could clearly see what a good property it was, and how well maintained (well, in the last few months anyway!). It was in a good residential area with all the usual amenities that most folk desire. The only thing that was quite distressing was that every time I showed someone around, I too could clearly see how very cosy, comfortable, stylish and elegant it was and, in truth, I still wanted it for myself! Of course, I just had to let it go – I'd made up my mind. But that didn't stop me from feeling a great sorrow about the home we had adored and had put so much love and energy into. Would he approve of me selling so soon? Several of my friends assured me that if I hadn't moved then, it wouldn't have been too long before I would have realised that my house was too big for just me and that the responsibility of it would eventually have depressed me even more, apart from the fact that it would make his absence a constant reminder to me. What they didn't realise was that I wanted to be constantly reminded of him. I just couldn't let him go.

It wasn't long before the house was sold and I could be on my way – but I had yet to conquer New Zealand House and immigration!!

2

With a tremendous feeling of urgency, I travelled to New Zealand House in London and handed in my application for a Resident's Permit. I assumed that a sweet little old granny like me, completely solvent, owner of property and in good health, with her only family already settled in New Zealand, would be accepted there and then on the spot. Perhaps not there and then, but I really didn't think it would take five months and ten visits to London to be finally accepted.

Of course, they needed to know absolutely every detail of my history. I even had to have a police report which rather alarmed me, since I was still very conscious of a speeding fine I had way back in the 1960s.

It brought to mind a rather silly thing I used to ask my girls when they were teenagers and were going out and about to various parties; 'What was it like? Good? Did the police come? It couldn't have been much fun if the police weren't called out!' Just joking with them as usual. But as things were now, I was feeling rather relieved that it wasn't true of any parties we had held in our house.

The whole experience caused me to reflect on my life. The biggest problem seemed to be my medical history. I had breast cancer thirteen years earlier and, naturally, they needed to be as sure as possible that I was completely clear of problems now.

I must tell you about the cancer experience which, of course, was very scary. I always had rather full breasts. In fact, I was so amply developed as a young teenager that I spent most of my time walking around with my arms folded in an attempt to hide my voluptuousness. I really wasn't too pleased to be so well endowed, and as I matured my opinion of big breasts didn't improve. The fact that members of the opposite sex always seemed to be speaking to my cleavage certainly didn't help matters. So I really didn't appreciate my prominent attributes. That was not until a lump the size of a hen's egg was found. From that point on my whole life changed.

I felt a tremendous guilt for not liking and accepting my body as it was, and, in a strange way, thought that I had been unkind to it. Faced with such a devastating situation, I quickly learnt to love my body and to be so very grateful for the life that I had.

I had an operation to remove the lump and radiotherapy, during which time I started to read self-help books. Books that discussed the way in which one can heal one's life – not just physically, but mentally. I had started on a journey of self-discovery. They say that a traumatic experience can trigger a 'wake-up call' and it certainly did for me. I read and read and slowly began to take on board all the advice that was being lovingly given. I tried to adopt a new way and, at the same time, remain positive about the changes in my life.

All seemed to be going well until, having finished the radiotherapy, I was told that since my cancer had been the most virulent kind, I would now need chemotherapy. At that point I felt utterly devastated. During further treatment, which proved to be very invasive, I needed the lenses of my glasses changed twice in one year, I lost a lot of my teeth, my fingernails constantly flaked and my hair thinned. But, I thought 'I'm still here!' and so continued to be very grateful.

Eventually, after a hysterectomy, I seemed to be on the road to recovery but one last thing was yet to happen. I got total alopecia and was left looking like a boiled egg! I don't think the exact cause of alopecia has been discovered, but I believe it has been associated with stress. However it occurs, I had it and it was something I just had to accept.

The odd thing about baldness is that we seem to accept it in men, but in women it's totally different and rather shocking. I had always had what people called 'pretty' hair, dark and naturally curly. Now, when I looked into the mirror I saw a total stranger staring back at me. Where had I gone? Although, with yet another trauma to cope with, I still remained cheerful and resolved to live my new existence with gratitude. As before, I kept thinking 'I'm still here!' and set about living each new day to the full. I began to really appreciate and understand a saying I had read printed on a calendar; 'Know the true value of time – snatch, seize and enjoy every minute of it.'

Eventually, I began to heal in body and mind and managed to turn a devastating experience into an enriching one. With regard to the loss of hair, I began to have fun experimenting with wigs of different styles and colour, and it was during that period that my daughter said something that I thought was rather amusing. I had, at that time, two young grandsons aged one and four. I had sat down with them and explained what had happened to me and had shown them the new bald me. Bless their little hearts! They had very seriously studied my head, tentatively touched it and agreed that I was still the same person as I was before, and that we all could still love each other. Nevertheless, my daughter had a request to make, 'I know you're being very brave, Mum, but could you choose a colour for your wig and stick to it? You are confusing the boys. Every time they see you walking up the drive, they say "There's a lady coming" while being totally unaware that it's you!'

As I have said, I used to be dark and curly, so now I thought it might be a good time for a change. I decided to turn myself into a blonde bombshell – or in my case a blonde bombsite! I chose a wig of straight hair in a subdued shade of blonde and thoroughly enjoyed walking around with the most elegant bob.

During the early years of wearing a wig, at bedtime the wig

would come off, the glasses off, the false teeth out etc, and I used to jokingly say to my husband, 'It's funny how I don't need to have a headache anymore!'

To this day, I have never made a secret of the fact that I wear wigs. I've always felt it my duty to tell anyone who remarks on my beautiful hair the whole truth in the event of either them or someone they know suffering the same fate. At least they might feel inspired to remember me and, hopefully, be encouraged.

'Life is patchwork – here and there scraps of pleasure and despair. Joined together, hit or miss.' (Anne Bronaugh.)

During this time of preparation for the move to New Zealand, I had started to ponder various aspects of my life. One which came to mind was my school days and on reflection, I realised I had been privileged to attend what I consider to be a very good school. As a teacher myself, I now realise how high the standard of teaching was. Not only that, but the whole ambience of the school was excellent. I can clearly remember the school motto, 'Enter to learn, go forth to serve' and also the school leaving song, which was very inspiring. I have always loved singing and can clearly remember belting it out with gusto – 'Go forth with God, the time is now. That thou must meet the test of youth, Salvation's helm upon thou brow. Go, girded with the living truth. In ways thine elder brethren trod, thy feet are set. Go forth with God.'

Yes, I enjoyed school and to prove it, I was made Head Girl! I hope that doesn't give the impression that I was a bossy-boots. I don't think I was; I just like things being done properly and in order. Colin liked the way I conducted myself so much that he used to say I could run a battleship! All this reminiscing caused the floodgates to open and thoughts of my husband to fill my mind again. The tears are never far away, ready to start flowing at any time.

I had to organise a memorial service for Colin and also write an obituary. I amazed myself by setting about this in my usual orderly fashion, being sure to include everything he would have liked in the service. I was so calm about it all, I suppose the dreadful realisation that death is inevitable helped me to know that I had to give it all my best shot; that the final farewell had to be as perfect as possible.

I sought permission to have the RAF flag draped over his coffin and to have a recording of an RAF marching band playing as he was brought into the church. Next, to have something by Sir Edward Elgar, then some choral music, and even a couple of his favourite songs that I used to sing – recorded, of course. I think it would have choked me to actually sing them there and then.

I found a wonderful piece of prose written by Bishop Brent; 'What is dying? A ship sails and I stand watching till she fades on the horizon and someone at my side says "She is gone". Gone where? Gone from my sight, that is all. She is just as large as when I saw her. The diminished size, and total loss of sight is in me, not in her, and just at the moment when someone at my side says "She is gone", there are others who are watching her coming, and other voices take up a glad shout, "There she comes!" – and that is dying.' At my request, the vicar included it in the service.

Of course, I was clutching at straws, unable to accept that it really was the end for him and seeking comfort for myself. Another piece, which I later found and now have on my study wall, is by Henry Scott Holland:

> Death is nothing at all. I have only slipped away into the next room. I am I, and you are you. Whatever we were to each other, that we still are. Call me by my old familiar name, speak to me in the easy way which you always used. Put no difference in your tone, wear no forced air of solemnity or sorrow. Laugh as we always laughed at the little jokes we enjoyed together. Let my name be ever the household word that it always was, let it be spoken without effort, without the trace of a shadow on it. Life means all that it ever meant. It is the same as it ever was; there is unbroken continuity. Why should I be out of mind because I am out of sight? I am waiting for

you, for an interval, somewhere very near, just round the corner. All is well.

You would have thought that the hardest thing for me to do would be to write his obituary, but it wasn't. I wanted everyone to know just what a wonderful man he was and how his life experiences had shaped him and, in turn, me. It spoke about his school days, his time as a medical student during the war and how he left his studies to join the RAF, resuming them later when the war was over. Also his time in Westminster Hospital (London) as a young doctor, and even how he rode down the steps of the Albert Hall on a motorbike. Naughty I know, but nevertheless it shows the spirit of the man, later to become a very well-loved and popular GP.

When I had registered his death and collected the death certificate, I felt as though I held his life, his history, in my hands and the responsibility was so great that I was determined to do him credit.

The vicar read all this out during the service. In fact, there were actually a few laughs along the way and many people remarked that, as far as one can, they had thoroughly enjoyed this funeral, this final farewell to him. He really loved balloons and one friend had actually tied some to his floral tribute, so the hearse was even adorned with yellow (his favourite colour) balloons! Yes, I think it all went as well as possible. We'd said goodbye as best we could.

Much later a dear friend, feeling that my sense of humour was returning, told me this joke:

When he knew he hadn't much time left, a husband said to his wife; 'You know the saying that you can't take it with you? Well, I'm going to. I want you to go to the bank and empty the account and, when the time comes, put all the money in the coffin with me.' At the gathering after the funeral, the wife was telling a friend about her husband's last request. Naturally the friend was horrified and remarked to the wife that she thought it was utter madness and surely she hadn't done it. The wife told her that she had done all her husband had requested and sent him on his way with the money inside the coffin, but with a slight amendment. When he died, she put all the money back in the bank and wrote him a cheque, which she then put in the coffin with him.

Thoughtful, eh?

3

A few months passed and spring arrived. I felt so annoyed with spring. How dare the sun shine and the whole place brighten up in anticipation of fresh new life and my dearest not here? As they say, 'life goes on' and in my heart I knew it had to, but it was so hard to accept.

A rather strange way to consol myself was to think of the great and talented of this world. Shakespeare immediately sprang to mind with all the wisdom and beauty of his prose and his magical use of language. I reasoned that if he had to die, leaving all that he had given to this world, I suppose we all have to, including my husband.

Colin had loved the garden and the first thing he did each morning was to walk out and closely inspect everything. We had built a pergola and planted a grape vine to cover the top, with a wisteria to creep along the front. That was approximately twelve years earlier and we had felt rather disappointed with it. The vine had not covered the top, leaving huge spaces where the sun crept in and the wisteria, although it had obligingly crept along the front, had never flowered.

Would you believe it? This year, now Colin wasn't here to see it, the wisteria was hanging in huge beautiful blooms and the vine was rampantly covering the gaps and, what's more, was producing bunches of delicate blossom which would almost certainly develop into succulent grapes. How could they? It almost seemed in defiance of his regular checking. I was so cross.

Another thing that strangely annoyed me was a row of holly bushes that we had planted along the front border of our garden. We had chosen a selection of various varieties in order to get a contrast of leaf formation and colour – we had even named our house 'The Hollies'. These, too, had stubbornly remained aloof from each other and had not spread out to make the interesting hedgerow we planned. Now, of course, they had suddenly had a tremendous spurt in growth and were stretching out their branches, embracing each other. It was all so exasperating.

In spite of all that, one small occurrence revived my failing spirits and that was the appearance of a beautiful butterfly which gently floated across my path. My husband had always altered words for fun. For example, alcoholic became 'alcofrolic', instructions were 'destructions' and now, here was a 'flutterby' to comfort me, something that immediately brought back fun memories of him and I felt he had sent me that to shake me out of the doldrums.

Knowing that eventually I would be leaving England to join my family the other side of the world, I planned to make sentimental journeys to all our favourite places in order to say goodbye. Naturally, I hoped to return for the occasional holiday, but for now, I needed to savour our special memories before I moved on.

One of my first visits was to the Cotswolds, Shakespeare country and all the most delightful surrounding districts. When I first met my husband, I had never been to the Cotswolds, quite amazing as I'm such a fan of Shakespeare. Colin was born very near Stratford upon Avon and, as a schoolboy, had regularly cycled to the theatre there. This suited us very well, because it meant that he could make his own sentimental journeys back home and I could indulge in my dreams of Elizabethan meadows, streams and maypoles and all the romantic ideas of a rustic life. During our time together we regularly visited and, although I was now retracing old steps alone,

I felt in my heart that he was there with me. It was a very bittersweet experience, but I simply could not have left without saying goodbye.

Another activity we used to enjoy was going to magnificent open-air concerts, held in the grounds of stately homes or castles. We would gather together a group of friends and book well in advance in order not to miss the event, praying for a fine evening. The atmosphere and camaraderie was so electric on those occasions. Meeting in the car park, struggling with deckchairs and picnic baskets to find a suitable place to settle and our delight in hearing the most wonderful music, played by a full orchestra, drifting across the meadow. Of course, while the orchestra played, the audience were enjoying their picnic and imbibing in gay abandon, so much so that by the time the finale of patriotic 'Last Night of the Proms' music came, everyone was ready to burst into song with great gusto.

I can remember one particular night when I actually disgraced myself, but thankfully we were alone on that occasion. It was during a festival in honour of Charles Dickens and was held in the grounds of Rochester Castle. I was always actively involved in this annual celebration and was regularly booked to give my talks about Victorian and Edwardian music hall, together with a little background social history of the times. Part of my contract with the council was to parade around the city during the day dressed in Victorian costume. Naturally, the tourists loved this – it was all so pretty, but what they never really understood was how very uncomfortable full Victorian costume could be, especially on a really hot day, when copious swigs of water were needed.

A wonderful Gilbert and Sullivan concert was held in a marquee in the castle grounds and later in the evening, when I was free, I was able to attend. A delightful little ticket booth, manned by a friend of mine during the day, had been erected at the entrance.

The concert was of course superb, but the day had been incredibly hot; water and also wine had been flowing. As the concert was coming to an end, I needed to relieve myself and began to feel rather uncomfortable. Nevertheless, determined not to miss a moment of this first-class performance, I told myself that I was a big girl now and could 'hold on'. Unfortunately, the feeling became more urgent than I could have imagined and, nudging my husband to follow, I made a sprint for the exit just as the final applause burst forth. By this time I was in such a desperate state that, dashing out, the only harbourage of privacy I could spy was the tiny ticket booth. Although tightly corseted and dressed in a huge hooped petticoat under my costume, I managed to squeeze in and squat down, but not without billows of silks and satins rising up around my face. Colin, of course, was horrified and was standing by the booth as the audience streamed out at the end. As he turned, he could see the exquisite feathers of an exotic bird rising above the front opening of the booth. These were the feathers of my headdress. He grumbled that if I didn't want to disgrace myself I should 'bob' down further in order to hide from prying eyes. I replied in a rather loud stage whisper, telling him to stop talking to an empty booth because it would look rather odd and would surely give the game away. By this time I think we were both in panic mode. I had to wait *in situ* until the marquee had finally emptied before I could winkle my way out.

That in itself wasn't a particularly pleasant experience, since by now the grass floor of the booth was flooded with hot, steaming water and was becoming exceedingly slippery. The whole experience was such a shock to me that, for some unknown reason, I burst into fits of uncontrollable giggles, which rather irritated my poor dear husband even more.

The next day, a group of us gathered for lunch and my friend, the one who occupied the booth during the day, told me that she had found an odd earring in there that morning which reminded her of a set that she had seen me wearing. Of course, it was mine and I claimed it expressing such surprise and wondering how on earth it could have been found in such an obscure place, all the time suppressing the nervous laughter that was still bubbling up just below the surface.

Later in the day, I actually told a couple of my closest friends the story of the feathers arising from the booth and all that had entailed; the relief of it all, the actual naughty deed, the rather pompous reaction of my husband, the struggle to get free of the booth, the discovery and claiming of the earring. We laughed so much that tears were streaming down our cheeks! I still laugh to myself whenever it comes to mind. They say that little things please little minds, don't they? One last thing to add to that story is the fact that the earring has now turned verdigris!

Another sentimental journey was made to Italy. We had both loved Italy above all other places and always took our holidays there. This particular visit came about when I was invited to attend a rather grand dinner with friends. During the course of the evening, the son of one of my friends announced that he intended to go to Italy for a holiday that year. I asked him where he planned to go and, as he didn't seem too sure, I proceeded to tell him about the various delights of the different areas and cities. I'm not sure whether my enthusiasm was infectious or whether he was slightly inebriated, but this lovely young man invited me to join him. Just imagine my delight, a sweet little old granny having the opportunity to visit a place she loved so much, escorted by a handsome, virile, thirty-two year old. Obviously, I wasn't going to turn that opportunity down and we arranged a meeting in order to discuss this further, after we each had time to reconsider the idea.

We both enjoyed intellectual pursuits – art, music, architecture, the history and beauty of the country, plus the wonderful food, wine, language and warmth of the people. And, what's more, we both felt we would enjoy it more in the company of a travelling companion. We knew each other well and it seemed a good idea. In fact, all our friends thought it would be good for both of us.

The next thing I felt we ought to sort out was what we would say about our relationship to people who we met during our travels. Although the age difference was very apparent, I felt the usual explanation of 'just good friends' always sounded rather suspect and I really didn't want to appear to be an aged dowager with her toy boy. In the end, we decided that I would pose as his mother's recently widowed sister – his aunt. I was in my element, enjoying all the delights of Italy, at the same time telling everyone that I was taking my nephew under my wing and expanding his knowledge of this wonderful place. I must say, it boosted my morale enormously and I swanned around in a very grandiose manner, looking out for my young man.

He, on the other hand, unbeknown to me, was telling the story of my recent bereavement and trauma and of how he was there to escort me in the capacity of a 'carer'. In a way he was, what with me being all fragile and him being a strapping young chap of over six feet tall. Anyway, we had a wonderful time and thoroughly enjoyed each other's company, so much so that much to my delight, we agreed that we would definitely do it again. Unfortunately, that wasn't to be. I was soon to move to the other side of the world and shortly afterwards he met a lovely young lady and eventually married, so no more escorted faraway foreign trips for me! In any case, I had an underlying, uncomfortable thought that I really shouldn't be enjoying myself so much when Colin wasn't here to enjoy everything with me.

I was also invited to Ascot, but decided to decline that invitation. Several years before I had been invited to the Royal Enclosure and, now, to join the hustle and bustle of the general hoi polloi didn't appeal. What a snob!

The year continued with the customary invitations given by kind friends, but sadly nothing seemed to erase the awful feeling of emptiness. Obviously, my friends couldn't be with me every single minute of every day and sadly many days passed without speaking a word to another human being. The odd times when I did actually enjoy myself, I still felt guilty in doing so. The memory of his suffering haunted me. I even felt cross with people that I met who were eighty and still enjoying themselves, while he was gone. I could still picture him in his coffin and remembered looking at his dear face and knowing he simply wasn't there, it was just a vacant body.

I would look at a photograph of him and think about how it had been taken only a year before he went, or just three months.

A photograph taken six weeks before he went showed him smiling in such a way that we could never have known what was ahead. All that and the continual stuffing of my face into his hat just so I could capture his smell was causing greater pain, but what else does one do? It's so hard to let go.

With the help of the photographs, I recalled everything we had done that last summer and I realised that we seemed to have made final sentimental journeys, particularly relevant to him. On reflection it seemed to have been a sort of winding-down process for him. We attended an Old Boys' lunch at his school, where he met many of his old classmates who are now eminent members of society. We went back to his university and were shown round the medical school. We even went to a couple of RAF reunions. In fact, we went to many activities that year that were of particular interest to him but I now know it must have been a tremendous effort for him. The photographs were showing me how weary he was looking. That, of course, made me sad because he had every reason to be feeling weary – he was old.

Although he was eighteen years older than me, because he was always so lively and such fun, I never actually acknowledged it. Why didn't someone tell me he was old? Now I am left with the awful regret that I might have shown more respect for his advanced years.

'Old age comes at a bad time.' (Unknown.)

'Remember your good memories, but live for today and keep the memories behind you.' (Jodi K. Elliott.)

With this kaleidoscope and turmoil of memories continually flooding into my mind, I arrived home from shopping one day to find a huge 'sold' sign hammered into the front garden of the house. It just about grounded me. It seemed as though everything I loved was lost. I walked into the empty house and just burst into tears.

A short while later, the telephone rang and the sweet voice of my little six-year-old grandson said 'Granny, where have you been? I rang you five times!' More tears, but tremendous gratitude too. I was still in this world and I knew I had to move on. Colin had enhanced my life so much, but I was still here, so were my family and I knew that this little fellow would soon be sharing all his news with me and I would feel the warmth of his enthusiasm.

I found this anonymous quote very helpful: 'Whatever you may have believed, whatever you may have done and whatever you may be in your life, it's never too late to change course and begin anew.'

4

The sale of the house went through incredibly quickly and I wondered if I had let it go too cheaply. Nevertheless, I really felt that I needed to get out of the house that I had shared with Colin and loved so dearly. Amazing, isn't it?

The new owners wanted to move in on the 10th December, just before Christmas and, at that point, I had no news of acceptance from New Zealand House or anywhere to stay, but anxious not to lose the sale, I agreed and everything went ahead.

I began to sort out and pack everything I treasured most. I gave my friends a lot of my things and I also gave a good deal to charity shops. The next question was the destination of the removal van. Should I put it all into storage in England or should I send it off to New Zealand, even though I hadn't yet received my acceptance? What a dilemma! In the end, I decided to be bold and send it ahead to New Zealand – after all, considering the time it would take to reach there, I could possibly have arrived myself. As the removals gentlemen were loading all the crates onto an enormous van, I couldn't help wondering if I would ever be reunited with all our treasures and what it would be like in an alien home on the other side of the world.

The last day of being in the house, when the removal firm had taken everything away, I walked around the empty rooms in total despair. It just didn't seem to be true. Colin was gone, the contents of our home together gone, and I was left here, in this totally empty shell, all alone. I was searching for a meaning because the whole world seemed so empty.

Looking back on it now, I really wonder why I just didn't take the easy way out and end it all for myself too, but I didn't. I didn't quite know how and I was scared I would hurt myself – ha ha! I suppose I couldn't have been that desperate. Change can be hard to take when the heart is aching; wanting things to be different but knowing that they can never be the same again.

I remembered the words written by Helen Keller; 'Life is either a daring adventure or nothing.' I decided on the daring adventure!

Being just a couple of weeks before Christmas, a friend offered me accommodation until I had a clearer idea about what I was going to do, so with only a couple of suitcases of clothes, I moved into her house not knowing if or when I would be able to make the journey to the other side of the world and my new existence. Everything I owned was gone, including my car, and I was still here! Utter madness!

I remember the first night in my friend's house as a complete mixture of emotions. I felt so relaxed being in a house full of family with all the buzz of the family's comings and goings. After having lived nearly a year rattling around in a reasonably big house, in total silence, the hubbub of family life was so very comforting. On the other hand, I am a chilly mortal who needs the warmth of central heating and the room that I occupied didn't seem to offer that comfort. I didn't want to mention it to my friend because she had been so kind in having me, but I became so cold that in addition to my usual nightclothes, I donned thick socks and a full-length woollen coat. That was in bed, but I also felt the need to ferret out of my suitcase several other garments to lay on top. I woke up early the next morning shivering with the cold, so I decided to get dressed and walk to the nearest shopping centre, which I assumed would be open due to the workforce arriving and, what's more, be warm.

I quietly let myself out of the front door, and was dismayed to find the rain pelting down. I don't think I will ever forget that walk to the shopping centre. It was something I would never normally have done. Usually I would have driven in the car and kept warm and dry, but here I was, freezing cold, battling against the rain and wind, to get there. I'm ashamed to say I actually cried all the way saying out loud, 'Look at me now Colin, this is what has happened to me.' Pathetic I know, but I really felt very fragile.

On reaching the centre, I sat, forlornly, on a seat in the centre aisle and as each worker arrived, I just looked at them and made the excuse I was so early due to the erratic bus service. In fact I began to wonder if that was what poor people have to do, those who have nothing but a meagre bag of possessions and no home or warmth, and my heart went out to them.

Another hurdle I had to jump was a final performance that I was committed to do at a local theatre. The word had got around and the theatre was filled with my dear friends and fans! And what an evening it proved to be. Everyone was right behind me, showing their appreciation and love. It was an absolutely amazing evening ending with a wonderful after-show reception, speeches and gifts. A friend had actually filmed the event so I had that as a poignant souvenir of the time when I was a 'real' person. To this day, I occasionally watch it and remember the thrill of it all.

Despite the cold, the two weeks leading up to Christmas passed in as pleasant a way as possible. I had actually started knitting again and during the visits to my many girlfriends, had inspired them to do the same. We heard of a group of ladies who had done something similar and had called themselves the Stitch and Bitch Club, so we identified with them and had a gossip, a laugh, a few glasses of wine and enjoyed each other's company. I began to thaw and enjoy the camaraderie of those wonderful meetings with my dear friends.

It was during this time that my eldest daughter, Jan, rang from New Zealand to tell me about a house that had just come on the market and which she thought would suit me well. She offered to act as my agent and buy the property in preparation for my arrival.

I wondered what to do – after all, who in their right mind buys a property without seeing it? – but this seemed to be a minor consideration at the time. I was feeling so lost and I was grateful that she was looking ahead and planning for my arrival.

'Change cannot be avoided. Change provides the opportunity for innovation. It gives you the chance to demonstrate your creativity.' (Keshavan Nair.)

My friends on the other hand were very worried about my actions. I was grateful for their care and concern, but I was prepared to take the gamble. I was stuck in England with absolutely nothing other than two suitcases, while all the contents of the house and the car were on their way to NZ. Add to that the fact that I was just about to forward cash to my daughter enabling her to buy a house I hadn't even seen – and still no acceptance from NZ House! No wonder they were concerned!

I'd like to point out an interesting fact. The property is in a village called Sumner, which also happens to be our name. Doesn't it seem rather a coincidence?

As Christmas drew near, I had to vacate the room at my friend's house in order for members of her own family to come and stay for the holiday, so I had to move on to another friend. These friends were pleased to help me, but had made arrangements to visit relatives over the holiday period. They were worried about leaving me, but, as I explained to them, in my mind I had cancelled Christmas, so would be very glad to be left all alone in my sorrow. As it happened, the house was warm and cosy, I was alone to ponder and cry, my knitting was growing at a great pace; throw in a bottle of wine and I felt I had all I needed right at that point in time. In fact, I only stopped knitting to raise the glass to my lips or to wipe the tears from my eyes.

'I feel sorry for people who don't drink. When they wake up in the morning, that's as good as they're going to feel all day.' (Frank Sinatra.)

And, as said in the odes of the Roman poet Horace; 'Mighty to inspire new hopes and powerful to drown the bitterness of cares.'

During those days, I couldn't help reminiscing about the wonderful Christmases we had shared together with family and friends. The first thing I had always loved to do was to decorate the house. I used to put holly with red ribbons intertwined up the stairway in the entrance hall and mount all the Christmas cards on them, which made a lovely colourful entrance for our visitors. I always preferred a tree dressed entirely in gold with angels blowing trumpets and that sort of thing. Rather reminiscent of Florence, I thought, and very elegant. Also, because we had a rather large mirror in the sitting room that reflected the whole area, I imagined it as a frozen pond. We used to go out into the woods and select a suitable branch that I sprayed silver, hung over the mirror, then decorated all in white and silver Christmas ornaments. In fact, my 'snow and ice scene' as I called it became the subject of great admiration and it was not long before my friends were copying my idea. What greater compliment is there than that?

'Christmas tree baubles only become valuable when they are veterans, fetched down every year from the attic, a little more worse for wear each year, but worth their weight in memories.' (Peter Gray.)

Trained as a teacher, I was full of ideas for Christmas quizzes and games and the house used to rock with squeals of delight and laughter. How we enjoyed ourselves, but that was just a memory of past times. More tears. I was beginning to feel really exhausted with all this crying and actually started to question if, perhaps, it was rather too much of me feeling sorry for myself! Whatever it was, it hurt!

My daughters rang from New Zealand and I was so heartened when my youngest daughter told me that there had been a 'memorial' Christmas tree in her nearest shopping centre and names of loved ones could be written on bow ties and hung in memory. She had put Colin's name there, which couldn't be more appropriate, since he always wore a bow tie.

More tears – how I wished I had shares in a paper handkerchief production company.

Christmas over, and another move on the agenda. I moved in with friends who lived on my road, so I had mixed feelings about being so close to 'home', as I thought of it. I wondered what Colin would have thought about all my moving around like a nomad. I'm sure he would have hated to see it happening, but at the same time he would be pleased to see that I was actually taking some sort of action.

We continued to stitch and bitch and before long we were all sporting beautifully home-made scarves and gloves etc. It was during that time that another friend of mine asked me if I would like to fill my time by doing some office work for her. Of course, I was delighted, so each morning she would pick me up, take me to her house, set me up with work for the day and supply me with a wonderful home-made cooked lunch, finally delivering me back to base at the end of the day. This was so good for me because it gave me some direction and something to occupy my mind. We'd sometimes drive out on errands and it was during that time that I made a rather silly mistake. She had parked her white car in a car park and I had rushed into a shop, only to discover that I had left my credit card in the previous shop several miles away in the next village. Of course, I was beside myself with worry and rushed back to the car, jumped in and shouted 'I'm in the shit now!' I then looked round to find a totally bewildered gentleman sitting at the steering wheel. In my fluster I had jumped into the wrong white car. The fact that my friend had moved her car didn't exactly help. I felt so embarrassed but thankfully both my friend and the gentleman were in fits of laughter.

Another time, with the same friend, it was my turn to laugh. She and her husband, plus a few of their friends, insisted that I went to a restaurant where they had 'look-alike artists' performing. I really didn't feel like going but was eventually persuaded.

I was so glad I did because I had such fun that evening. When the artist came on, he was impersonating Freddie Mercury and was exceedingly good. Half way through his performance, he asked if it was anybody's birthday and if it was, would they come up to the stage area? A young girl went up, he hugged and kissed her and everyone sang 'Happy Birthday'. It all looked so jolly, warm and comforting and I began to think 'I could do with some of that' so when he asked if there was anyone else, I put up my hand. I stepped up into the lights, had a hug and a kiss and congratulations all round and felt human again for a while (thank goodness I didn't have to tell him my age!).

On arriving back to the table in a fluster of excitement, my friend said, 'I thought your birthday was in May!' 'Yes it is,' I confessed, 'I just wanted to feel the warmth and camaraderie of the gathering heightened.' They all fell about full of laughter at my naughty escapade and I must confess that when I arrived home, I felt rather ashamed at what I had done, and perhaps how much wine I'd consumed! One thing I did recognise that night was that I have always been lucky in my humorous reaction to whatever life has handed me, so at least I had that working in my favour.

Time to move on again. It was only a matter of five weeks after I had vacated my house that the housing market took a tumble. The gentleman of the house told me that it would never have realised the price I got for it in the present climate and since he was an estate agent and a qualified surveyor, I was confident he would know. That, at least, was rather comforting.

It was just a week afterwards that the long-awaited acceptance from New Zealand House arrived. I instantly booked a flight into the unknown.

Here is something that I think is incredible. On the 10th January 2005 I read my horoscope in the *Daily Mail*, written by Jonathan Cainer. It said:

Gemini May 22 – June 22. Something is starting to work – more or less. You don't, though, feel inclined to see yourself as victorious. You feel more as if you have stumbled (as much by chance as skill) upon a vaguely viable plan. You have a solution that is probably going to be 'good enough'. You are reluctantly resigning yourself to an arrangement. So, your mood is not so much one of 'Hooray, we're off!' It's more 'Oh well, here goes.' Yet the venture that you are embarking on is not, actually, a second-best option. It is the perfect path for you, right now.'

Just to add to the above, I collected my visa from New Zealand House on the 14th. What an incentive to release the old and make way for the new.

5

On arriving in NZ, I stayed with my daughter Jan and son-in-law, Andrew, until the 1st April when my new home was to be vacated. I sincerely hope that it being April Fool's Day wasn't an omen!

After only a week in NZ, I have learnt so much. There's a saying which I feel is so typical of the NZ attitude to life – it's simply 'As long as it takes'. For example, their non-existent timekeeping is surprisingly something that I have adapted to very quickly. I looked at my watch the other day and realised that it was the first time I had done so all day. The time was 2.15pm! Amazing, considering I was always timekeeping at home. The shops tend not to open until 10.30ish – I'm sure in England a tremendous amount of trading would have been done by that time.

I have, painfully, learnt not to sunbathe. The first time I sat out in the sun, even with protection, my legs were so burnt they were actually painful. The fact is that my English skin is far too fair and sensitive. This was confirmed by a kind lady in a shop who quite surprised me, since we were total strangers. She came up to me and said, 'Take my advice, dear, and don't go out in the sun with that beautiful English skin of yours.'

Of course I was extremely grateful and could see her point. To be frank, I had already observed that the more mature New

Zealanders have faces that look as though they need ironing! Lines and wrinkles are in abundance here.

Apparently, because the air is so pure and unpolluted, the rays burn to a much harder degree. Even Jan, a young English rose, has developed a ruddy complexion so with all that as evidence, together with the kind advice I've had from the locals, I shall definitely be shunning the sun in the future.

As for the temperature, they have UVI indicators in municipal buildings and along the roadside. These are huge coloured circles with segmented semi-circles that have an indicator pointing to the appropriate temperature. This really serves as a good warning about the dangers of too much sun – as I've already experienced.

Another kindly lady actually crossed the road to say to me, 'You're English, aren't you?' When asked how she knew, she replied, 'No-one dresses like that around here.' I suppose to be dressed in rather smart city clothes in a dear little old seaside village was rather inappropriate!

I must say that I am surprised by the fact that they all know I'm English even before I open my mouth. I don't have a 'Made in Britain' sign tattooed on my forehead.

'Life isn't about finding yourself. Life is about creating yourself.' (Unknown.)

'Life is half spent before one knows what life is.' (French Proverb.)

Is this my chance, at sixty-two years of age, to change my identity?

One of the most pleasant things I have discovered so far is the café culture. There are attractive open-air areas for relaxing, chatting, eating and drinking, but a degree in English Literature might be an advantage when reading the menu. For example: 'A huge, colourful bowl, filled with steaming hot coffee, with milk, as smooth as silk. Topped by our world-famous liquid art, plus a side of marshmallows.' All that literary effort for a cup of coffee? By the way, the artwork was an impressive pattern floating on the top of the froth, rather like the patterns of the English corn circles. Reading the main menu was quite tiring. Why couldn't they simply say 'fish and chips' without telling you the name of the fish, where and how it was harvested, how it was cooked, plus the dressing and accompanying vegetables with details of their origins?

One weekend Jan, her husband and I drove to Hanmer Springs to meet up with my other daughter, Sue, and her family from the North Island, for the eldest grandson's (Chris's) eighteenth birthday. The drive was absolutely delightful and, on the way, we passed the Waipara area, famous for its vineyards. Hanmer itself was a very quaint little town with luxurious motels and lots of old wooden shiplap houses with pretty little gardens. The most important feature of the area was the naturally heated thermal pools.

The luxury of an unhurried soak in the hot mineral pools is an experience that I think will linger in my memory. It was absolutely lovely. The open-air complex is in an alpine setting and the locals assure you that to enjoy it even more, you have to experience it when the temperature is low and the surrounding mountains are covered in snow.

Conveniently, the many bubbling pools vary in temperature and therefore you have the choice of how hot you want to be. The interesting thing is that once you're in the pool, you just sit back and relax on the rocks but the water is incredibly buoyant, so all 'dangly bits' begin to float. I'll make no comment on the male species, but I, as a woman, was rewarded in as much as my own sagging bits immediately perked up!

Looking around, I couldn't help pondering how interesting the human race is. Apart from the diversity of mind and intellect, bodies vary enormously, and, in my opinion, we all looked like great slugs, sunning ourselves on the rocks – quite a revolting sight really.

In addition to the usual holiday activities like miniature putting, there were many outdoor pursuits of the daring kind. Sue and Jeff chose to ride on a jet boat at high speed along a river. You could hear the screams echoing all around the canyon and when they eventually got off, they staggered up the hill with jelly legs and wet hair!

Another activity was bungee jumping. When asked by my daughters if I fancied having a go, I simply informed them that I would rather stick to my usual laxatives ... One thing about being of a mature age is that you don't have to feel a sissy if you don't participate. I was very happy to observe with a drink (water – honestly!) from an elevated terrace.

The boys decided to go for a spin on a motorised go-kart safari. This might sound quite tame, but the terrain involved all sorts of thrills and spills. They too arrived back looking slightly shell shocked and the worse for wear – but nevertheless delighted.

We all wanted to stay together in the same motel, so it was necessary for my eldest grandson and I to share a double room. Since I had been a major feature in his upbringing, this presented no problem. Naturally, with my wicked sense of humour, I couldn't resist having some fun with him the next day.

We all gathered together for a special birthday brunch and while the crowd was noisily enjoying the occasion, I quietly leaned across and whispered in his ear, 'I bet you will be the only boy who can say he slept with his granny on his eighteenth birthday!'

On a more sober note, sadly it was then Colin's anniversary. Was it really only a year ago? How so much had changed during the year – it all seemed a lifetime away. I tried to reconstruct our marriage and I felt so sorry I didn't keep a diary. The only way I can trace our time together now is by photographs.

As ever, I found some comfort from a few remembered quotes. 'Yesterday is history. Tomorrow is a mystery. Today is a gift – that's why it's called the present.' (Eleanor Roosevelt.) I simply love all her quotes ... so profound. So I resolved to make the best of my 'present' and try to stop lingering in the past. As Abraham Lincoln said; 'Most folks are about as happy as they make up their minds to be.'

Jan and Andrew then went away for a whole week, so I had complete peace – just me ... and the cat! Jan had been moaning that I was beginning to fill up my bedroom with goodies for the new house, so I was able to buy whatever I liked and squirrel the stuff away like nuts in anticipation of a winter famine! I also collected

A LEAP INTO THE UNKNOWN

my car from storage and at last I had my very own passport to freedom. It was so good to have my own transport, but I must say the NZ bus service is fantastic. Not only do they have buses scooting regularly all over the place, but at each bus stop they actually have an electric board which tells you exactly when the bus is due to arrive and how it is progressing. I remarked how wonderful I thought it was to a local who very proudly informed me that their service was the best in the world. A true fact. I spent a whole afternoon in my new house while the present occupants were at work. I am more enchanted with the house than I thought possible for a batty old English bird who buys a house without even viewing it.

Unfortunately, much to my surprise, although being a truly delightful residence, it had suffered badly at the hands of the previous owners and had all been rather neglected, so I will have lots to do restoring it to its former grandeur. The interior needs completely redecorating, all curtains, blinds and carpets replacing and the garden, which at present resembles a jungle, needs urgent attention. Nevertheless, I really think I can be happy here. As a teacher, something else I have noticed since being here and which greatly pleases me is the weekend activities. As you drive past any recreation field, it is buzzing with activity. Youngsters are learning cricket, soft ball, rugby etc. In fact, whole fields are sectioned off for the various activities, so that hardly an inch is out of use. Also, driving along the beach, you can see beach volleyball being played – not by just one or two people, but many. The NZ way is to get out in the fresh air exercising, competing, team building and generally having a good time.

I have joined a croquet club and am told that I have a good wrist action. I rather fancy myself as an elegant Edwardian lady gently tapping the ball, but, as it turns out, they say I have a mean whack of the mallet!

For all those who are interested in dressmaking, knitting, greeting card making, jewellery making, or any other craft activities, I have never seen such craft shops before. I went into one a few days ago and spent at least an hour there, just looking around at all the interesting activities one can do at home. I suspect this is a throwback from the pioneer days I spoke about earlier, when mass produced items were not available and the women just had to get down to creating things themselves – think of the wonderful patchwork quilts of the New Englanders. It's all going on here. Dare I say I'm knitting again? Naturally, what with a little tipple to help the creative juices flowing, I have to check on all the dropped stitches the day after the night before!

Creativity is a combination of intuitiveness, enthusiasm, flexibility, intelligence, independence and initiative. Anyone can have creative ideas, but trusting them and putting them into practice builds creative character.' (Dr P.W. Buffington.)

It's lovely here, but I think it is safe to say the honeymoon period in NZ is over for me. Things are beginning to bug me!

NZ people are so incredibly nice, warm and friendly, which my British reserve is finding hard to accept. For example, everyone – the bank manager, the customs officer, the assistants who take your details in the shops, anyone you might ring regarding services, just about everyone – calls you by your Christian name. Now, that seems far too familiar to me. I am used to being respectfully addressed as Mrs Sumner – only my friends can call me Marie.

Next is their accent (by the way – they seem to love mine). It's all beginning to grate on me. I long to hear an English accent and I've even resorted to watching UK TV whenever I need a quick fix. The only trouble is, it's episodes of sitcoms which are years old and rather dated now.

And another thing, the saying they use when something is OK – 'good as gold'. 'It's good as gold.' This immediately brings back memories of my childhood, when my granny used to say to me that I was as good as gold – sickening, isn't it? I have mixed feelings about being reminded of my 'goodness'.

As Mae West said; 'Too much of a good thing can be wonderful.' And we all know what she was referring to!

Unfortunately, I'm not sure whether being as good as gold has rather limited my development and outlook and just how much I must have missed. I want to be naughty, but it's too late now!

'Youth is a blunder, manhood a struggle, old age a regret.' (Disraeli.)

I'm certainly regretting being 'as good as gold'! I'm beginning to suspect that NZ has been greatly influenced by the US, which isn't surprising when you look at the map. All the shop assistants ask you, in a very sweet way, 'And how's your day going?' to which you are expected to reply, 'Fine, thanks.' Then, as you leave they say, 'Enjoy the rest of your day!' My British reserve really can't cope with this level of friendliness from strangers and I'm beginning to feel tempted to reply, 'Absolutely bloody awful. My husband has left me for a barmaid, my children are all on probation, the bank manager has frozen the account and the bailiffs are due this afternoon. But apart from that, fine thanks.'

As a teacher, I find I can't resist studying children and my observations are that as infants and juniors, they are like the Waltons family – all pure and good and sweet. Yuk! Then, as they become teenagers, they turn all cocky and full of psycho-babble. I recently overheard a teenager talking about having 'quality time' with his parents. The boys here aren't much different from the UK version of Neolithic man, with one-syllable grunts, and the girls go round in a flock like birds – all twittering. Their form of dress is pretty amazing. Tops that just about cover their boobs and finish just below them – boob tubes – and their pelmet skirts hang somewhere on the hips, exposing vast expanses of flesh. By what I've observed, sales for belly-button studs must be pretty hot here. Don't I sound my age?

Young boy to Mother: 'I want to have some body piercings!'
Mother: 'Oh no, you're not!'
Son: 'But everyone has got them.'
Mother: 'Well, no son of mine is going to have them.'
Son: 'But Granddad's got them!'
Mother: 'Yes, but that was due to World War Two!'

The weather is something I'm finding really difficult to adjust to. It's so odd. I always thought our British weather was unstable, but this is something else! Let's look at the seasons first. As you know, everything is the other round from the UK here. Winter in England is summer in NZ. Winter in NZ is summer in England. Regarding English summer, I think it fair to say that it is unpredictable, but NZ weather is totally bizarre! Although NZ summer is a lot warmer during the day, it cools very quickly at night, whereas it has been known to be warm enough to sit outside until the early hours in a good English summer.

English winter is cold and damp whereas in NZ, winter is crisp and dry and very often sunny.

Jan has told me that they often sit outside in suitable clothes, enjoying the winter sun. So far, so good, but being a remote island we are exposed to the most powerful winds. Now, it is these winds that can change everything in summer. You could be basking in the warmth of a summer's day when quite suddenly an icy wind blows through. These winds can be extremely strong. I don't need to remind you how difficult this can be for a wig wearer!

Strong gust! Major wig alert! Poor me! I'm having to do my Jackie Kennedy scarf routine. In addition to that, if the wind is not too fierce and I leave off the scarf I am faced with another problem. Because synthetic wigs don't naturally fall back into place when blown upon and tend to remain standing on end, I have to watch out that I don't look as though I've just stuck my finger in a live socket!

The southerly winds are cold and bring bad weather and rain, which I've witnessed falling down horizontally – yes truly, horizontally. The easterly winds, which come directly off the sea, are the most hated and are extremely cold. The northwest winds are warm, but when they are blowing you feel as though you are under a hairdryer. So that tells you how hot they can be. Regardless of the season, Christchurch is renowned for having all four seasons in one day so I think it's fair to say you don't know where you are. My advice to any English visitor is to come with a suitcase of clothes for all seasons. It's early autumn here at present and one day I actually changed my clothes three times. The beginning of the day was overcast and nippy – ah, autumn, I thought – so I dressed in warm clothes, which included tights. By noon, I was back in summer trousers and by 3 p.m. I had to resort to shorts and sandals. Quite frankly I'm changing so much in every way, I'm afraid that I'll eventually leave my wig off, start chewing tobacco and adjusting my crotch!

When I was in the UK I became quite alarmed about the political situation and terrorism, so when I landed here, I felt a sort of relief. After all, we are so far from absolutely anywhere, I sort of hoped that the terrorists haven't noticed us.

Well, that's been shattered now, with fears of a new danger. The New Zealanders seem to think that the chances of a terrorist attack in the UK are on a par with a serious earthquake here. I'm stressed because slight rumblings happen frequently, even here in Sumner. And, to top it all, the local newspaper ran an article last week saying that NZ could have a tsunami if there was an earthquake, so they were asking people to join the local civil defence society in order to train in dealing with such an event. I am supposed to be in paradise, but nothing is perfect.

As it happened, just a few days later, I experienced my first earthquake! Of course you've heard the expression 'Did the earth move for you, baby?' For the first time ever, it did! It happened during the night and it woke me up. The bed started to shake, rattle and roll and all I could do was just lay there hoping for the best. Luckily Jan and Andrew were home from their trip, so I didn't feel as alarmed as I might have done had I been in the house all by myself. At least I know what to expect in future. In the morning they told me that it had been a mild one, so I've yet to find out what a more severe one will feel like.

Now I have my car, I've been able to get around more freely. Incidentally, collecting the car was an odd experience too. When I first saw it waiting for me, I felt like embracing it. It's such a little darling and it had come all the way from the other side of the world to be with me. It really felt like a friend had come. It felt as though Colin was near me again, after all, it was the last thing he bought for me, just four weeks before his demise. He had only ridden in it a couple of times. I felt a strange sort of closeness to him which made me feel so happy.

Now I have the car, I have discovered that apart from the malls within the city, there are seven other shopping malls on the outskirts! Imagine that! Isn't it fantastic?

I've actually been driving in the centre of Christchurch as well. Christchurch must be the only city left where you can still actually park in the streets and it looks as though it might be easy to navigate since it is built in the grid system similar to the US cities, but, there are nine one way streets that run across the centre, so if you inadvertently miss a turning, as I have done several times, you find yourself stuck in a circuit from which it is very hard to escape. I'm now becoming quite immune to all the beep-beeping I seem to cause. In extreme cases of causing annoyance, I simply play the part of a confused batty old English bird and it seems to work quite well. Plus, the accent helps – they love it.

Since I had a map of the city centre enlarged to A3 size and then highlighted the one-way roads in different colours according to the direction, I'm beginning to show signs of improvement. I drive everywhere with the map on the steering wheel, but it's OK since the car is automatic and needs very little operating anyway.

Sumner has just had a wine and food festival and, of course, I forced myself to go! As you might expect, there were tents all around with goodies to sample. They had great bales of straw in the centre that you could sit on. The atmosphere was great and I passed several pleasant hours imbibing and chatting with the locals. I am beginning to know quite a few people now, so that was a good afternoon.

I've even bought a cookery book! I'm not a natural cook but this book has been especially written for busy people, so all the recipes seem to be very easy and straightforward and yet interesting, so hopefully I will be able to cope. I must confess to being just a little tired of toasted sandwiches!

The date when I take over the house is drawing near and I am busily arranging for tradesmen to call and discuss various jobs that need to be done. One such job is the bath. The bath in this place is a big free-standing claw foot antique but, unfortunately, like the rest of the house, in need of tender loving care. Jan said she would have it out and have a modern bath installed (trust the young) but I rather like it and since I have made several enquiries about it, I have discovered that it must be at least fifty years old and very sought after, so I have decided to have it resurfaced and painted gold on the outside. The work can't be done on site, so they collect it, take it back to a factory and the whole process takes three weeks. Naturally, it is quite an expensive operation, but I feel it will be worth the effort. I imagine the first time I use it, I shall feel like a Hollywood starlet, very grand, wallowing in such a bath with the customary glass of champagne, of course.

6

When my young friend Andrew and I went to Italy last year, it was his first visit and he was so impressed with its splendour that the word 'Wow' was one of the most common in his vocabulary. After a while, we began to judge places by their 'wow' factor. This is very prevalent here in NZ. Many vistas are so astoundingly beautiful, with such an intensity and depth of colour, that if one viewed them in a book or professional photograph one might be forgiven for thinking they had been enhanced.

I have been very happy this week because friends from the UK – Margaret and Duncan – are here on holiday and we have been out and about on trips of discovery together. On our first trip out, we drove along the coast of Pegasus Bay to the wine area of Waipara Valley, thirty minutes drive north of Christchurch. Its latitude equates to that of the south of France in the northern hemisphere. To the east, Waipara is separated from Pegasus Bay by a range of hills that protect it from the cooling winds of the Pacific. To the west lie the Southern Alps, from whence the region's hot northwest winds derive – its sheltered position resulting in a very prolonged ripening period.

The day was hot and to lunch in one of the vineyards seemed the obvious thing to do. Vineyards in NZ are usually beautifully landscaped, with large restaurants and sweeping gardens for dining out. Wine tasting is encouraged. Of course, I forced myself to be sociable and tried a few! This particular vineyard had named their wine with a musical theme, so I felt I just had to try Aria, Maestro, Prima Donna and Finale. Of course, Prima Donna was my favourite.

After a delightful couple of hours of eating and drinking we tumbled back into the car, and drove to the nearest little village, Amberley, which being on the coast had a wonderful expanse of beach to enjoy. There was only one other family there. It's quite odd really; you begin to wonder if there has been a bomb scare or something and you haven't been told. And what a wonderful opportunity to go skinny dipping! Of course, we old codgers didn't, we were just content to settle down and snooze. Big mistake – the sun is so intense that, before you know what's happened, you find yourself severely burnt. Consequently, and in spite of the fact that I have been warned several times before, I have spent the last few days in great pain with huge red lumps up my arms, legs, across my chest and round the back of my neck. So now I've truly learnt my lesson . . . I hope! We were glad to arrive back to the sanctuary of my daughter's garden.

Jan's garden is a sight to behold. It has been professionally landscaped and is utterly fabulous, mainly due to the fact that it is the size of a pocket handkerchief. There is not an inch free and it is full of the most luscious plants you could imagine. Added to all the wonderful vegetation, there are two fantastic waterfalls. It's so grand, it almost looks municipal!

On Wednesday, we went over the mountain at the back of Sumner to the historic port of Lyttelton. As you drive over the top of the mountain, the view has 'mega wow' factor. Lyttelton Harbour is beautifully scenic and very near Christchurch. It is on the Banks Peninsular, which was once a volcanic island – Lyttelton Harbour is the sea-filled crater of a volcano that erupted 11 million years ago.

The day we visited an enormous cruise ship had docked, so that was a sight to see. It made me wonder when the container with all my worldly goods will arrive. We drove round the coastline to a place called Diamond Harbour, passing many other little harbours on the way. After lunch, back once more to Sumner. Although not far from Sumner, these trips out take all day because there is so much to see.

We had dinner in a restaurant on the edge of Sumner Bay. It was very entertaining, because we could see people windsurfing and parasailing on surf boards – and falling off! It looked great fun to do and was very addictive to watch.

On Thursday, time for a ride on the Gondola. The 945-metre Austrian Doppelmayer Gondola operation gently lifts visitors to the top of the Port Hills, almost 500 metres above sea level. Unique 360-degree panoramic views of Christchurch, the Canterbury Plains and Lyttelton Harbour unfold as you rise to the summit complex, on the rim of Christchurch's famous extinct volcano. Absolutely amazing.

After a pleasurable few days, we arranged to meet up again in Napier in the North Island for a very special Art Deco Festival. Margaret and Duncan moved on to visit family who were living further south. A couple of years prior to my arrival, very good friends of mine had emigrated to NZ to be with their son. At the time, I had no idea I would be joining them.

They had moved further south to a place called Alexandra and wanted me to visit – my trip proved to be a kaleidoscope of experiences. It being the first time I had travelled within the country, I was stuck by the friendliness of the 'natives'. People are constantly acknowledging your existence and asking how you are etc. If it were the UK, you'd feel rather wary of such attention, but here it seems so natural. When I arrived in Queenstown, my friends Alfred and Barbara were there to greet me. We drove through the mountains to their hometown of Alexandra, passing the villages of Cromwell and Clyde.

The area of Central Otago is famous for its history of gold mining and this is reflected in the real feeling of antiquity one experiences. It seems rather reminiscent of the Wild West in the 1800s, the landscape we see depicted in the 'cowboys and Indians' films.

A LEAP INTO THE UNKNOWN

The scenery is spectacular and the grandeur of the mountains is humbling. The area is now a thriving centre for farmers and fruit growers and has a booming wine industry.

As we drove towards Alexandra we passed two waterfalls, one called Roaring Meg and the other, Gentle Annie. Apparently they had been named after two barmaids who had worked in the saloon in 1862.

Alfred and Barbara have a beautiful house, actually built on the side of a mountain over an old gold mine! I was quite lost when I first entered, since they have several levels of accommodation and I wasn't sure where I was going and what I was going to find behind each door as I opened it. Even the sitting room was split-level. It also had two balconies on different levels, so we had the choice of where to sit according to the position of the sun. I was billeted in a bedroom at the very bottom of the property which had a cave built into the mountain hidden within one of the walls. To be quite frank, I found in all rather eerie, and I didn't relish sleeping down there – all alone!

On the night of my arrival we went to a Masonic Meeting. The ladies gathered together for a chat in an outer room while the men conducted their business in private. I thought how civilised this was since, in the UK, the wives are not included in any way and usually stay at home. After the meeting, the wives were invited into the actual temple because several of the men were being awarded their twenty-six-year service badge. I was interested to hear a short talk by each of them about the principles of Masonry and how things hadn't changed much from the time of their joining. One gentleman mentioned how, back in those times, they used to make sure that all the widows of the village had firewood during the winter months and how that continues to this very day. Obviously, in such small communities, they know and care about each other. Everyone is so incredibly warm and friendly that Barbie and I remarked that it reminded us of *Stepford Wives*.

The next day I was taken to the local bowls club, which was in the most tranquil setting. Everyone, yet again, was extremely friendly and as I watched them at their sport I thought how easy it would be to slip into genteel retirement – but not yet.

The Probus Club were due to meet the next day and had been let down by a speaker, so I was asked to give one of my talks. All this was off the cuff, since all my notes were still in the container. They assured me that they would be just as interested in hearing stories about my life! So I made a few notes of the highlights of my teaching and entertainment days, and threw in a few songs for good measure. Much to my surprise I had a tremendous reception and was rather horrified when I was introduced as a famous English actress and singer. Apparently, some of the people present had seen me on the UK television in NZ and had actually believed I was 'big time', so I was very much aware of not letting them (or myself) down.

'Do what you can, with what you have, where you are.' (Theodore Roosevelt.)

I managed to fill an hour on my favourite subject – me. Many wanted to speak to me afterwards and all were very complimentary, so I felt quite satisfied. During my talk I mentioned my last performance in England which Barbara very cleverly called 'The Last Night of the Poms'! and so, with that, the evening concluded very successfully.

The next day, since the temperature has constantly been well over 100ºC, we decided to go swimming. This posed a problem for me because, since an injury to my shoulder, I have very limited use of my left arm. With the use of just one arm I am only able to swim around in a circle! Nevertheless I had a wonderful time aqua jogging instead. Not being very 'sporty' I didn't know about aqua jogging and was delighted to find it suited me very well because it's really good exercise without too much exertion. You have a float thingy strapped to your middle and you walk, run or 'bicycle' in the water. Happily, just about my level of physical exertion!

One day we visited a delightful little town called Ranfurly, which like many NZ towns has some lovely Art Deco buildings from the streamlined Jazz Age of the 1920s and 1930s.

The senior citizens in NZ certainly know how to enjoy themselves. Apart from Masons, Probus, bowls, croquet, bridge, Mahjong, swimming etc. there are dancing classes!

Barbara, although over sixty and somewhat overweight, took me along to her tap dancing class. Although I obviously couldn't join in, I thoroughly enjoyed it. The music was jolly and I was able to indulge myself in one of my favourite hobbies – people watching! The class was made up of the usual scrawny six to eight year olds, all bobbing around with great enthusiasm, but also mature ladies of the grand size that our famous English artist Beryl Cook depicts. All tapping away. I must say that the Beryl Cook ladies far outshone the young ones with their elegance. It was so heartening to see ladies of such a size and age still having a go and not allowing life to pass them by.

Another great activity is line dancing – which I never in a million years thought I could enjoy. The music can be so infectious, very different from my usual choice of string quartets ...

To enjoy line dancing you have to think of hillbilly country folk having simple, unsophisticated enjoyment. Although I must say, I had a bit of a culture shock when one of the songs mentioned a 'coyote' and the dancers all yelped like a dog. In spite of that, I really got into it, so goodbye Marie Lloyd, the famous Edwardian singer whose songs I used to sing – hello Dolly Parton. I have got the blonde hair and the boobs!

Another lovely social event was a BBQ at Lake Dunstan. Since the UVI indicator was a good warning, we sat in the shade of the trees and enjoyed watching people swim or fish.

'If you want a place in the sun, prepare to put up with a few blisters.' (Abigail Van Buren.)

It was an idyllic spot and I can see why New Zealanders describe their land as 'God's own country' and call it 'Godzone'. We visited another lovely place on the side of a lake called Wanaka. The splendour of the mountains and lakes, plus the long list of adrenaline-inducing outdoor activities make it a favoured tourist destination all year round. As you tour around NZ, especially in the South

Island, you begin to notice the names of places. There are numerous Creeks, Gullies, Junctions – all, again, reminiscent of the Wild West. During this little holiday I have seen places so remote that I'm sure even Wells Fargo wouldn't have been stopping there.

I love the peace and quite of it all. Even the cafés and restaurants, which often have pounding music in the UK, have lovely tranquil music playing so you really can enjoy a leisurely meal. Occasionally you are faced with modern day living, for example in Queenstown, which I would say is a 'young person's' place and could be described as 'vibrant'! Queenstown, on the northern shore of the serpentine Lake Wakatipu, is the epitome of the big-budget resort town awash with tour groups and plenty of hustling for the tourist dollar. There's great skiing in winter and plenty of summer pastimes too. Most activities are centred on the lake and the many nearby rivers, with white-water rafting, sledging and jet boating, or for the very brave, bungee jumping or tandem parachuting! The town is also well equipped for more earth-bound pursuits, like winesipping, boutique-browsing and dinner-digesting, all of which are more to my taste. If you value your own space, it's not for you; the whole place is abuzz with humanity of all kinds.

Alfred and Barbara gave me a wonderful time and every day brought fresh delight. I must mention the last meal we shared. We went to a vineyard, which had a restaurant, gift shop and cheesery – all of the highest quality. I jotted down two dishes from the descriptive menu:
1   Vine smoked rabbit with rillette, a roasted courgette and fava bean salad, baked chestnut-crumbed labneh cheese, and lemon vincotto dressing.
2   South Island hare loin with porcini, duck liver and almond tart, with merguez mossmushroom, apple and pancetta salad and papardelle.

In spite of all that, I must say that I still really miss my frozen food packet meals from Marks and Spencer. How I wish I could order some food parcels to be sent!

On returning home, I found that I would have some time alone.

A LEAP INTO THE UNKNOWN

Jan and Andrew planned to fly up to the North Island for a Rod Stewart concert and they wanted me to drop them off at the airport and bring their car back home. Jan's car is one of those huge four-wheel drive station wagons, built for towing horse boxes etc., so you can imagine my trepidation in driving it, but I had no excuse since it was automatic! I did it and when I eventually reached home, I had gained a considerable amount of confidence. I rather liked the feeling of grandeur, sailing along in such an elevated position, so I continued to use it for the rest of the weekend. The only unfortunate thing was that I felt I needed a parachute to get out of it and safely on terra firma.

After a few days alone, I had time to reflect and I started to think more in depth about this wonderful country and its people. Why am I so instantly feeling at home here, safe and happy? What makes this place so interesting? We have two islands, so diverse that I feel somewhat inadequate to describe them to you – nevertheless, here goes. I have gathered a few observations, which I hope will help you to capture a 'feel' for the place.

Let's look at it geographically. It sits alone midway between the equator and the South Pole, and is one of the world's purest and least polluted environments. It doesn't even have any poisonous snakes or other such predators. The North Island is subtropical – so think South Pacific – sandy beaches, luxuriant shrubs and swaying palms. The South Island is mountainous, untamed, virtually an inhabited terrain of forest, fjords, lakes and waterfalls. So here we have two islands, which I am now discovering seem to contain all the ingredients of the many European countries that I have visited. For example, the beauty of the Italian coastline and the lakes, the magnificent mountains of Switzerland, perfect for skiing, the fjords of Norway etc. It is an amazing conglomeration of geographical ingredients.

From a historical point of view, at some point the Maoris, a Polynesian people, heroically canoed across the Pacific Ocean and settled here in this paradise. Then, in around 1642, European sailors spied NZ (notably our own Captain Cook) and started to infiltrate the country. We can now see a history similar to the US, with the persecution of the Native Americans. The Maoris were eventually so overwhelmed that they are now a minority.

But, while feeling very sympathetic towards them, as one would feel toward the Native Americans, I cannot help but feel greatly impressed by the courage of the early settlers. The British became the governing body (hence the Union Jack set in the NZ flag) but other nationalities also came, such as the Dutch and the Chinese gold miners, so we begin to have a mixture of cultures.

The majority of dwellings in NZ look like New England – pretty little wooden shiplap dwellings surrounded by garden fences embracing delightful gardens, ablaze with colour. Then there is the elegance of the stylish Art Deco towns of the 1920s and 1930s. The modern buildings that are mushrooming in NZ are absolutely incredible – each one with its own unique character.

It's interesting to see how the country is developing, and yet the customs are still strongly influenced by those of the early settlers. For example, one is expected to generously share one's talents for no payment; a plumber does a job for an electrician and vice versa, no money changes hands and it balances the need to survive as comfortably as possible.

Also, one never goes visiting without taking a plate! The plates usually consist of one's special recipe for apple pie or such. At first, I didn't understand that tradition so when asked to take a plate, I felt so sorry that they were short of plates that I offered to take many, although all empty!

Jan has told her friends that she expects to be entertained when invited and not expected to bring a plate when she visits them. Likewise, when they come to her, they can expect to be entertained without bothering to prepare a plate. As it happens, they are all in agreement, so perhaps she is going to change history!

I've tried to paint a picture of my impressions and I sincerely hope I've done the country and the people justice. One last comment to make – I now understand why so many young NZ backpackers travel to England. They are seeking out their roots. For example,

A LEAP INTO THE UNKNOWN

Jan's husband's grandfather was originally from Burnley in Lancashire. Since many NZs are descendants of English families they travel to the UK to capture the essence of their origins. When visitors arrive and see our heritage and the magnificent buildings, they are gobsmacked! For example, Rochester Castle and Cathedral, built all those years ago by the Normans – that's proof of 'real' history! That, together with the delights of wicked London, leaves them reeling at what's hit them and they want to savour all that the UK offers, just as we Brits do their country. It's a case of 'the grass is greener'. All this excitement and yet, I have noticed, they all return to Godzone!

I have flown to the North Island to attend the fabulous Art Deco Festival in the most wonderful town, Napier. On the edge of Hawkes Bay, Napier had an earthquake in 1931 measuring 7.8 on the Richter scale. It was a massive earthquake by world standards. Of course, a disaster of this nature brings with it fires and water supplies are disrupted, a total collapse of infrastructure. It was devastating and many lives were lost. Consequently the town was rebuilt soon after the earthquake in 1931. All the buildings are of the architecture of that time, all very ornate and grand and beautifully preserved. It really is an amazing town and it was so good to be able to walk around as a tourist and enjoy all the activities. The locals were in 1920s costume and looked very pretty indeed. Brass bands played the music of the era, with Jitterbugging dance lessons on offer and a soft-shoe shuffle for those less energetic. There was a real Art Deco wedding, a 'bathing belles' competition, and many more activities.

My favourite was 'The Picnic'. Groups of people brought their pagoda-type tents to the municipal gardens and set up their picnics. They had carpets, drinks trolleys, silver teapots and cocktail glasses, silver decanters, horn record players – everything as it should be. All of this had to be genuine. They sat there enjoying their stylish picnics while we, the tourists, filed past oo-ing and ah-ing. One group of jolly young men even had a notice saying: 'Any young flappers welcome'. There were street entertainers, my favourites being a group of men dressed as the Keystone Cops – they had a robber that they were continually chasing, and kept getting muddled and falling over each other, hitting themselves with their truncheons! It was hilarious; they must have been black and blue at the end of the day.

There were also wonderful strolling Barbershop groups. The ladies looked very colourful in their drop-waist fringed dresses, floating chiffon scarves, long beads, cloche hats or feathered headbands, fringed shawls, pointed toe-bar shoes, fox furs, long cigarette holders, Chinese sunshades, etc. and the men looked equally delightful in their rowing blazers, cravats, boaters or Panama hats and two-tone shoes. I couldn't help thinking it all looked far more comfortable to wear than the Victorian costumes I had to adorn for the Dickensian festivals in Rochester.

The music was such fun too. Strains of 'The Sheik of Araby', the Charleston and wonderful ragtime jazz were so infectious that everyone was soon jigging around in the streets. The major attraction was the parade of vintage cars. There was well over a hundred of them, all different makes and colours and all in perfect condition, driven with such pride by their owners. When I was speaking to one of the stewards, he told me that the parade was shorter this year because they limited it to cars no later then 1939. Apparently, the reason that NZ has so many vintage car societies (nearly every major town has one) is because it is only in recent years that the government has allowed car imports, so anyone who had an old car just had to keep it in good condition and continue to use it. It was all so very beautiful and I really enjoyed it.

From there, I travelled down to Wellington to visit my youngest daughter and family. It was good to see Sue again and her new home – very big and grand! The two younger boys seem to have settled well in their new school. The eldest, Chris, who had just turned eighteen, was enjoying some free time with a visiting friend from the UK, so they were out and about golfing, bowling, swimming etc. I think his parents will be glad to see him settling down when the visitor goes home! Sue and I enjoyed a few days together, relaxing, gossiping and shopping.

I must say I was quite glad to get on the plane back to Christchurch.

I felt quite weary after all that. I now have to be patient and wait another month before I can eventually move into my own place. In the meantime, Jan's friends continue to be very welcoming and invite me to BBQs and such. Although I'm very grateful, I shall be glad to make friends of my own age, since I feel slightly uncomfortable with the frothiness of their existence.

I wonder if I should tell you a rather shocking little story! (Well – it was for me.) I had a visit to the stable to watch Jan have a riding lesson. I have discovered one big set back – in the country there are no public loos! Since I had been drinking copious amounts of water I was badly in need of one. Jan had earlier, with no bother at all, simply lowered her jodhpurs and squatted down assuring me it was 'country ways'. Of course, that is not my way, except in an emergency such as the 'booth' business after the G and S concert! I was getting desperate, so in order to relieve myself I crawled up to the trunk of a tree with long flowing branches. Not being very practiced in such matters, I soon found myself in difficulty. I don't seem to have the balance I used to have. Nevertheless, once started one has to keep going! My aim was slightly askew, which made me somewhat flustered. On finishing and in my haste, I quickly stood up only to find the wretched branches of the tree fighting with my wig and winning. With my wig dangling from a branch, I was truly panicking.

Having untangled myself, I staggered out of my shelter with a skewiff wig and very wet feet. To add insult to injury, I accidentally trod in a huge mound left by a horse earlier, so my wet shoes instantly became muddy. I never thought I'd say it, but I think I really ought to be exchanging my high heels for wellies sooner than I expected. Only to go riding, of course. I'm determined not to stoop to shopping in them.

So much for country ways. I felt rather shell-shocked by the experience, but worse was to come. On reaching the sanctuary of the car, I was so hot and bothered that I removed my wig and wiped my head with a tissue – yes, you've guessed – the same one that I had used earlier under the tree! Was I glad to get back home to a soothing hot bath!

But before I end this chapter, I must tell you this odd story. On the main road leading from Christchurch out to Sumner beach, there is a section that has been cordoned off with railings. Jan pointed out that a seagull had laid her eggs there, the young had just hatched and the authorities were protecting the spot even though it was on a busy section of the highway! How's that for kindness? Some locals have now added two little houses for the babies.

It's all so cute, but I feel sure it could cause an accident because you simply can't resist having a look to keep up to date with their development.

7

Jan had her first horse trials of the season and entered dressage, jumping and cross country. We left home at 7 a.m. and arrived at the venue about 7.45 – I was stunned to see so many four by fours and horse vans queuing up to enter.

Horsey people are a breed of their own! The minute they park, they jump out and with great enthusiasm proceed to groom their horse. This entails giving them a good brush down, combing the tail and, with something resembling a tin opener, hooking mud out of the hooves. I even saw one lady painting her horse's hooves, which I suppose isn't much different from we humans using nail varnish for a special event.

By the way, you sure do need real money to ride. Jan took me to a tack shop full of the gadgets one needs for a horse. That expense is on top of the stabling, feeding and the actual cost of buying the beast. It brought to mind my early days of marriage, gathering together things for the household.

Apparently, for just a simple egg, one needs a pan for boiling, a frying pan, a saucepan for scrambling, a poacher, a coddler, a separator, a whisk, a slicer – the list seemed endless. As a result, I decided after a while that life was far too interesting to spend so many hours in the kitchen – and what for? Only to have a bunch of uncouth beings (namely, the family) demolish all my efforts in three minutes flat.

Incidentally, I've already noted the gear I shall need to bring in future. A chair, a blanket, an umbrella, a picnic hamper, and, just in case it all gets too much for me, a crossword book and, of course, a bottle of wine! Need I say more?

The horses were immaculately groomed. Unfortunately, the owners were quite different. Scruffy old jeans, wellies and dirty old anoraks. Not quite as grand as I had seen on the television but when all the dirty work had been done, I witnessed the most amazing metamorphosis. These ugly caterpillars transformed into the most stylish butterflies, clad in their cream jodhpurs, shiny black boots, formal tailored jackets and protective riding hats. They, together with their trusty steeds, looked fantastic. Soon the field was awash with stylish young women looking very superior with their straight backs on their mounts, who were trotting, running and jumping all at their command.

It wasn't long before I was informed of my duties, which were to drive the car to various places between fields, to polish Jan's boots when she was saddled so that they were gleaming and had no tufts of grass, and to wipe the spittle that accumulates around the horse's mouth and nose. I really began to feel part of the scene and to be relaxed until I spotted a St John's Ambulance lurking, which served to remind me just how dangerous this hobby can be. When I remarked upon it, the riders were quite proud to tell me their stories of various accidents and broken bones.

Jan did exceedingly well in the dressage and jumping, and according to the updates was in line for a ribbon, but in the last event, the cross country, she jumped really well into the water, sailed across, but went to the side of the two flags instead of in between, so lost all she'd gained. Poor thing, she was so disappointed. As for myself, I had brought a book to read in the car but was so captivated, I didn't even open it.

'The old woman I shall become will be quite different from the woman I am now.' (Anonymous.)

The day I was to take over the house dawned – the 31st March. How relieved I felt to know that I had a home of my own again. I've been extremely lucky to have family and friends who have taken me in, but 'there's no place like home' and it's been four months for me without one.

Although I loved the house in England, this house is something special. To begin with, the location is marvellous. I can look out of any of the windows and see the mountains and the sea, and every time I drive into Christchurch I see all sorts of seaside activities being enjoyed along the way.

The house is so different from any other I've lived in. It has a grand tiled entrance hall, leading into the sitting room. The sitting room has glass concertina doors all along one side, which can be completely opened up, and there are beautiful terracotta tiled steps leading down into the side of the garden.

The dining area and the kitchen are open plan and have French doors that also open out onto a raised deck, leading down into another area of the garden. There is also a double bedroom on the ground floor, very nicely situated next to a shower room and lavatory. I'm especially pleased with that since it will enable any visitors to enjoy their own privacy.

There are so many attractive features. The entire lower floor and all other woodwork throughout the house is in rimu, the native wood, and fortunately our English pine furniture blends in and suits it well. Unfortunately, there have been a few problems in the sitting and dining room areas that have proved to be difficult to resolve. For instance, with all the concertina doors there are two whole walls missing, so where does one put furniture and pictures? And I have those in abundance!

Upstairs there are a further three bedrooms, the main bedroom having French doors that lead out onto a delightful balcony overlooking the garden. There is a wonderful walk-in wardrobe. Yippee! Somewhere to house all my 'skinny person's' new fashions. The bathroom has the magnificent free-standing claw footed bath, which I love. And a feature that I really like is the landing which is open plan and runs along the length of the house. With four large windows, it will make an excellent study area. I might even keep a kettle and some coffee up there, so that I can pad out of my bedroom and check my emails each morning before going downstairs and starting the day. It certainly is an interesting house but (why does there always have to be a 'but'?) the previous owners have not taken care of it and it is in a very sad state.

No doubt you are familiar with the idea of 'the little black book'! When I was young, mine was filled with 'Husbands' and 'Lovers' – I think not – but it sounds interesting, but as I grew older, it became full of doctors, dentists and chiropodists. Now I've reached the stage where it is full of painters, plumbers, electricians and gardeners. I couldn't help thinking how sad it was until I met the painter, plumber, electrician and gardener – not the motley crew I had anticipated, but handsome, young men all eager to serve my needs. My needs are actually to restore the house to its former glory, so I spent a whole week watching the rippling muscles – ooops – I mean supervising all the work that needed to be done.

The day dawned when the container with the entire contents of our home arrived. I can tell you now that unpacking your life's collection of possessions is a really daunting experience. You can't believe you could have packed and brought such junk all the way around the world! And yet, I love my junk, it all holds special memories. In fact, I had a few very pleasant surprises – stuff I had completely forgotten about. Naturally, I was absolutely delighted to be reunited with 'my life' and setting about finding places for all my treasures transpired to be a very satisfying task.

'One doesn't recognise in one's life the really important moments; not until it's too late.' (Agatha Christie.)

I always said that the house I had left in England was my most loved home but the house I have now is an utter delight. I love it to bits, and I feel very privileged and happy to be here. I don't need to tell you that Colin would make my happiness complete, but I cling to the idea of life after death and the fact he might just be here, in spirit, with me.

I tried to make the best of things and managed to place a few pieces but seeing the 'Golden Age' antique tea set that I had arranged on the Welsh dresser, visitors advised me that it wasn't the best position for such beautiful china due to the earthquake situation. Although not too serious so far, the tremors can shake things to such an extent that they fall and get broken. I value all the beautiful possessions we collected over the years and wanted to have them around me, so it posed a great problem. Ever resourceful, I'm pleased to say I soon resolved it with copious amounts of Blu-Tack!

Yes, I think I am going to settle nicely here.

As Samuel Taylor Coleridge said; 'Do not fear to hope . . . Each time we smell the autumn's dying scent, we know that primrose time will come again.'

Within four days of moving, Sue and the family descended from the North Island. Naturally, I was pleased to see them – I can't say I was anywhere near ready for visitors, but they didn't mind a bit and were a real help. It also confirmed how very convenient the house is for the family in general, as well as the visitors I am promised from England.

During the time they were here it was Wesley's fifteenth birthday. We all wanted to go out for a meal that evening, but he simply preferred to have a pizza sent in, so that was just as enjoyable. In fact, since he can now handle a screwdriver, he was extremely helpful during the week and seemed to enjoy reassembling pieces of the furniture that had been taken to pieces. Mind you, he was well rewarded with pocket money, so was very enthusiastic. Sue and Jeff helped with unpacking and by the time they left, I was more or less sorted out.

I felt I ought to show them some of the highlights of this area and first stop was the Christchurch Gondola with its 360-degree views of Lyttelton Harbour, Banks Peninsular and the city of Christchurch, backed by the grandeur of the mountains. Another touristy thing to do is to go for a ride on the Christchurch tramway. Trams were part of Christchurch city in the latter parts of the last century, with horse-drawn and steam trams running services to many parts of the city. The electric tram was introduced in 1905 and remained in service until 1954, when they disappeared from the Christchurch streets. Due to the dedication of the Tramway Historical Society and the vision of the Christchurch City Council, the 1905 trams were brought back again, and they are an absolute delight. A ride on them rather reminded me of Judy Garland and 'The Tram Song'.

The vehicles seemed just the same and I got an overwhelming urge to burst into song. The family were only here for a week, so there wasn't too much time to take them round and about, since they were generously spending much of their time and energy helping me, but they were able to get the feel of the area and they saw the house, so they were quite happy.

Another difference between NZ and England is the television. I've never been a telly-addict, but have enjoyed the occasional programme. Here, I simply don't bother because it is awful! All that over-excited, fast-talking type of presentation. As we are surrounded by mountains, the reception is dreadful, so we have to have cable. Actually, I quite enjoy watching all the old films that I just didn't have the time or opportunity to see in the cinema so that's good at least. Nevertheless, I'm rather concerned that I can't seem to tune into anything on a regular basis, like the news and the weather. No doubt I'll soon get it sorted out, but for the time being I feel a little lost. On the other hand, I'm totally unaware of what's going on in the world outside, so I suppose it's quite a comfort living in a cosy cocoon.

Since I am an avid reader, I am shocked by the price of books here. They are more than twice the price of anything in the UK. I suppose the reason being that they are mostly imported from the UK, so one has to pay for that. I have discovered a wonderful bookshop and spent a fortune already, so I can't visit there too often. Perhaps I should start frequenting the second-hand bookshops. At least they seem to be plentiful, and now I know why!

A LEAP INTO THE UNKNOWN

I hear from friends in the UK that the weather is cheering everyone up with glimpses of spring. Here it is autumn. The leaves are changing colour, falling off the trees and it is getting colder. The majority of NZ houses don't have central heating – it's a new feature which has only been introduced in the last few years. Most places have wood burners. The minute I clapped eyes on the monstrosity in my sitting room, I knew I had to do something about it. I just couldn't imagine, in the depths of winter, having to clean it all out first thing every morning and, with arms full of logs, prepare it for the coming day. Yuk! As a result of this, during the time all the jobs were being done in the house, I had a gas burner installed. Jan had wanted me to have central heating, but the locals had advised me that gas burners were excellent, so rather than have all the upheaval of yet more work before I moved in, I decided to give it a go.

The last few days have been wet, windy and very chilly, and I have had the jolly old gas burner going at full pelt, and it's been perfect. The pipe from the heater runs up from the ground floor to the upstairs landing and successfully heats all the area above too, which in turn, takes the chill from the other rooms.

It's quite interesting because the general smell from the outside world reminds me of Guy Fawkes night in England. When I look out, I can see the smoke curling up from the surrounding houses. They, obviously, still have the old-fashioned log burners. I pity them, cleaning out the ashes and carrying in the logs each day. I suppose they are used to it, but since I just can't bear being cold, I had to make a more civilised arrangement. Thinking about things I miss most about the UK, I suppose right now it would be appropriate to say central heating. Yes, I long to drift from room to room without a care in the world, instead of making a hasty dash from point to point. I'm getting wise and I lay out the clothes I intend to wear the next day before going to bed so in the morning, after my customary bath, I simply jump into them and I'm not too chilled. Of course, this is only in the mornings. I still have to face a day of changing temperatures, so it's far more complicated. I have just experienced such a day of complications. It started as a typical autumn day, slightly chilly, therefore warmer clothes. By 11 a.m. much warmer, so one layer discarded. By 2 p.m. everyone is sitting out on their decks wining and dining. So where am I? Still huddled indoors pretending it is autumn.

On the whole, I thought I had settled in pretty well, that was until I unpacked the last of the boxes containing all the CDs (500 of them) that Colin collected. All that wonderful music that we had enjoyed together. So many memories came flooding back, together with many tears, that I felt just as devastated as though it were only yesterday. It's still so very painful. I feel I have everything and, yet, nothing. It's so hard sometimes.

So, you see, I am truly trying to carry on. With regard to the wonderful free-standing claw foot bath, it has gone off at great expense to be resurfaced. I told the gentleman that I wanted it painted gold on the outside, since I intended to have a white and gold bathroom. He seemed quite surprised but went along with my idea. So far, so good. The bath was delivered and installed and looked absolutely fabulous, and with my little gold cherub ornaments cavorting all over the place I felt very happy. My intention was to fill the bath with bubbles and slip in with a glass of champagne, just like a Hollywood starlet. The big day arrived when I intended to christen the bath in all its splendour but much to my amazement, I couldn't bring myself to crack open the bubbly. It seemed so very decadent. I was concerned that Colin, in spirit, would be wondering what was happening to me. Nevertheless I decided not to skimp on the bubble bath, which I generously squirted into the water. Gingerly climbing into the bath, what a shock I got! It was far bigger than I realised and the first thing that happened was that I slipped completely under, causing tidal waves to gush over the ends, and generally flood the floor, which, I might add, had just been laid with new lino. Not to be deterred, I decided to leave the mopping up until later so I could slowly let myself relax and indulge in the sheer luxury of such an item. Unfortunately, I forgot that I was only five foot three inches long and the bath must be at least six foot, so my little legs and feet had nothing to cling on to. This caused me to float, completely out of control. I tried to gain control, but I discovered that the sides were much higher than I realised, making them difficult to cling to. As you can imagine, all this found me desperately thrashing around like some poor hooked fish.

I eventually managed to cope with it all and began to settle down to what I usually enjoy doing in the bath which is to take time to cogitate and plan, but all I could think about was boats. Yes, boats! I thought I could get a collection of tiny boats to sail around while I'm bathing. Seemed like a good idea to me until I glanced down at the two mountainous objects protruding from the vicinity of my chest, and I realised that they would soon run aground. So that idea was shelved, as would be the boats. By the time I had coped with mopping up the flooding and everything else, I felt so sweaty and unhinged that I really needed another bath. In the end, I decided I just couldn't face it so soon after all the trauma of the first. Of course, I just accepted it all, just as we all have to do when things don't go exactly as we planned, but I'm determined to enjoy my bath in the future.

'Noble deeds and hot baths are the best cures for depression.' (Dodie Smith.)

Further to my whinging Pom comments about New Zealand, I thought I might start telling you of the things I miss most about England, some with tongue in cheek. So here goes with the first, which is Morris Dancing. I really miss the jolly music of this ancient tradition. The virile, robust gentlemen, skipping and waving their ribbons in gay abandon. Here, the nearest activities to that are Maoris, striding forward, legs straddled as though they have had an unfortunate accident, waving spears and waggling their tongues. Oh, how I long for my favourite sort of men, the ones who skip, prance, wave pretty coloured ribbons and at worse, hit each other with sticks!

8

It has been lovely for me lately. My old friends Alfred and Barbara from Alexandra came to visit me. Naturally, I took them around and about, showing them all the delights of this area and they were duly impressed. They live in an area less populated than this that lacks a lot of the amenities I have here. The first thing that amazed them, as it did me when I first came, is that Christchurch has seven wonderful shopping malls dotted around the outside of the town!

Little thoughtful things never fail to surprise me. For example, we ordered three cappuccinos and the decaffeinated had 'decaf' written in chocolate. Obviously the young lady had taken a shine to Alfred and put a heart on his! I love these coffees and have even bought myself a coffee bean grinder and a cappuccino coffee machine, but as yet not put it all to the test. As you know my enthusiasm for any activity in the kitchen is nil, but at least I'm thinking about it!

While they were here I took them for a drive around the many inlets of the harbour and on to Akaroa, about one and half hours from Christchurch. The road eventually climbs to the top of a volcano and then descends to many rural bays and beaches. It is the unique site of the only attempted settlement by the French in NZ, so their influence is evident with the French street names and many historic buildings. When eating out, French cuisine is an obvious choice, but we had good old-fashioned fish and chips. It was quite the best I've ever tasted.

With hardly any traffic on the road to Akaroa we still managed to get caught in a jam, only this time it was a cattle jam! The cows were everywhere and we just had to be patient while the herdsman tried to control his stock from a sort of motorised buggy. All very amusing.

I think a quote about friends would be appropriate here; 'Of all the things which wisdom provides to make life entirely happy, much the greatest is the possession of friendship.' (Epicurus.) I can confirm that, since I've certainly felt the need to keep in touch with my old friends on arrival here, knowing no-one else.

Another quote that I particularly like is; 'A friend hears the song in my heart and sings it to me when my memory fails.' (Anonymous.)

Sometimes I feel I've lost the sweet memories I had and can only focus on the traumas of losing Colin. Although I certainly don't want him out of my mind, I really look forward to the time when I can, at least, think of him without the tears flowing. I have now joined the Royal Over-Seas League, which holds meeting in Christchurch every month, so I am at last beginning to get out and about. But I still feel very reticent about mixing. Sometimes I feel like a wounded animal that just wants to cuddle up and centre my attention on healing my broken heart.

My introduction to the Royal Over-Seas League proved to be fateful. I was performing my 'Last Night of the Proms' act dressed as Britannia in England, when a NZ lady in the audience came up to me afterwards to congratulate me on the performance. She was so enthusiastic that she told me that if ever I was in NZ I would be most welcome to visit the Royal Over-Seas League. I think the outcome of that casual invitation is so interesting, especially since I was totally unaware at the time that I would eventually be living here.

Which leads me to think, once again, of what I miss most about the UK. It might seem a very simple thing but it is having the post delivered through the letterbox in the front door and being able to pick up the post from the mat still in night clothes. Here in NZ, we have letterboxes at the end of the drive and have to walk out to get the mail. Not at all nice in wet and windy weather and I don't think the locals would be too impressed with my well-worn nightwear and the thick football socks I wear in bed.

I remember the first time Colin and I slept together, he said, 'I think you need to go to the chiropodist, dear,' to which I replied, 'That's not my feet you can feel, it's my football socks!' Since I wasn't exactly love's young dream, I thought I might just as well be myself – socks and all!

As a result of the effort of walking down the drive in all weathers, I tend to forget that I might even have mail and, when I do eventually remember, I seem to have a bulging post box.

It was my birthday on the 24th May and I had a lovely surprise. Jan and Andrew took me out to dinner in a village about thirty minutes drive the other side of Christchurch. When they called to pick me up and I walked out to the car, I found a chauffeur standing by the open door of a white stretch limousine. What a surprise! While sipping champagne on the way to the restaurant, I think I could be forgiven for feeling rather indulged and very grand. On the return journey, the chauffeur took us around the night spots of Christchurch and I must say I was tempted to do a queenly wave to everyone, but with Jan closely watching me, I thought better of it. She seems to think I am OTT at times. I don't know why!

Since I can hardly believe that I am actually sixty-four years old now, I started to ponder about life and how quickly it passes. The obvious thing was to search through the books of quotes that I have collected over the years, and to find what other people have had to say about getting old and old age itself. There were so many that seemed so suitable that I have decided to list a selection and, if any of them seem relevant to you – tough luck! You must be facing the same dilemmas as me! Here goes:

'As you get older, don't slow down – speed up. There's less time left.' (Malcomb Forbes.)

'Don't eat healthy foods! You need all the preservatives you can get.' (Unknown.)

A LEAP INTO THE UNKNOWN

'Have a good time because you are only old once.' (Unknown.)
'You can't control the past, but you can ruin a perfectly good present by worrying about the future.' (Unknown.) One which I really need to take to heart just now.
'If not now – when?' (Unknown.)
All very interesting and worth consideration, don't you think?
I've recently found out how the NZ health service differs from the English system. You pay for it as you need it. Every time you visit a doctor it costs approximately £15-20 pounds in English money, plus extra for any prescription that you might need. In England, you make an appointment to see the doctor and then start a procedure of being referred to a specialist doctor if needed, which, of course, is very time consuming. Here in NZ, you have complete and easy access to any doctor you may wish to see; they are all simply listed in the telephone book.
This has worked really well for me because I have been able to go directly to the very doctor I need – a dermatologist. New Zealanders go frequently for what they call a 'mole map', a check for skin cancer. With past history and the fact that my skin just cannot tolerate the sun, it is essential that I keep a check on this. Already I have developed horrible little warty things all across the top of my chest. So, the sensible thing to do was to trot along to the appropriate doctor. He, of course, was most charming and assured me that he could rid me of all that was bothering me. This absolutely amazed me, because my chest resembles the craters of the moon. He also noticed the brown spots that seem to appear on the top of elderly hands, and informed me that he could get rid of those too. In fairness to him, he did mention that after the treatment, it would all look worse before getting better.
By the way, have you ever thought what an odd paradox it is that a doctor asks you to undress behind curtains to save your modesty and yet draws them apart with a flourish, revealing your nudity and embarrassment, when you have done so? It doesn't make sense to me. After a few minutes shivering and beginning to wonder if I had made the right decision, he returned with what I can only

describe as one of those spray cans you use to spray the greenfly off roses. He explained that the contents would burn off the offending warts and brown spots. It didn't hurt at all and I soon began to get into it and search around for anything else that I thought could do with a squirt. He explained that they would form a scab and fall off within a couple of weeks, leaving my skin all young and beautiful again. Naturally, I felt quite happy about that until I caught a glimpse of myself in his mirror – I looked as though I had a severe case of measles and had to return home looking like this. What hadn't occurred to me was the fact that I would continue to look like this for the next two weeks! Jan actually fell about laughing when she saw me. I thought, 'She may be laughing now, but her time will come!'

Actually it all turned out to be a worthwhile procedure and I have resolved to return for a 'respray' whenever necessary. So happy am I with it all that I began enthusiastically thumbing through the telephone directory in search of anything else I might need. I did wonder if there was anyone who could do something about the loss of my hair, but although I didn't mind the 'fly spray for roses' technique, I didn't fancy walking around with a bag of manure for a turban!

All this talk about the trials and tribulations of ageing and I now have to admit that I am still struggling with the bath! I just can't seem to lower myself into it without causing a huge tidal wave. I really don't want to resort to one of those chairs that real geriatrics seem to need, so I am still racking my brains for various other solutions to the problem.

Last weekend the English Lions rugby team arrived to play the world renowned NZ All Blacks! New Zealanders are totally into rugby, so you can imagine what a great occasion it was. So many Brits came to support their team that every possible accommodation in Christchurch was full, so a huge cruise liner was docked in Lyttelton Harbour for the duration of the event and served to billet the Brits. Jan and I went for a drive over the mountain to see it and it really was a spectacular sight. It stood way above the water-

A LEAP INTO THE UNKNOWN

line and was gaily lit up! The little town of Lyttelton had risen to the occasion and had a Festival of Lights, which I suppose is the NZ way of brightening up the winter months. There was a jolly street party, music and copious amounts of booze, so everyone seemed to be enjoying themselves.

As it happened, the All Blacks slaughtered The Lions, but the reports on the match magnanimously said that The Lions were weaker because they were made up of several rugby teams from different countries (meaning England, Ireland, Scotland and Wales) and obviously hadn't had the unity of continual practice with each other. I often wonder why England is referred to as the United Kingdom. When you consider it, we are hardly a united kingdom any more. Anyway, the whole atmosphere was very genial and as I drove out the next day I noticed that a poster that had read 'All Blacks v The Lions' had been altered to 'All Blacks v The Pussycats'!

Incidentally, last weekend was a busy one for me. I did a two-day art course, which I thoroughly enjoyed. The first day was basic traditional watercolour painting (my preferred style) but the second day was something quite different. The tutor told us we were going to have a 'wild' day experimenting with colour. To tell the truth, I'm not into 'wild' days and therefore was feeling slightly reticent about it, but nothing ventured, nothing gained – so I threw myself into it.

First, we had to slosh buckets of water onto the paper, next go wild with splodges of different colours thrown on randomly and, finally, tilt the paper in all directions so that the paints were running and dripping all over the place. The tutor promised that something magical would happen and, sure enough, it did!

He said that we would see a subject matter appearing which we would be able to develop into a picture. Mine was a hillside in Tuscany with ramshackle old buildings surrounded by tall Lombardy poplar trees. Since I had mainly used royal blues, emerald greens and bright magenta, the whole effect was amazing – a wonderful explosion of vibrant colour. He then proceeded to show us how we could develop the picture further by erasing bits and pieces of colour here and there, to give fantastic contrasts and depths to the picture.

You know what it's like when you create something; you can never feel totally satisfied that you've done a good job. On the contrary, I must confess to loving what I've done, the subject matter simply jumped out at me as he had promised and it's zany and interesting, simply bursting with colour. I'm overjoyed with it. I had responded to his suggestion and as a result produced a masterpiece.

Being the kind, sharing person I am, I offered to have it framed for Jan's sitting room, but she regretfully declined saying it would look much better in mine! Do I have to read between the lines here? However, with great gusto, I announced that I would free myself from the shackles of traditional painting and create many more of these fantastic pieces of art, and circulate them amongst my nearest and dearest, so that I am 'hung' in all their sitting rooms. At that point Jan seemed to have some sort of fit, coughing and spluttering, which seemed to end with her collapsing onto the nearest chair and making a funny noise which seemed to resemble a sort of choked hysterical laugh. Poor thing, not being as artistic as me, she didn't seem to appreciate my wonderful creativity. Ha Ha!

Now I know how talented I am, I feel the most overpowering creative urge bubbling up inside me and I certainly intend to share it with the world.

'Abstract art? A product of the untalented, sold by the unprincipled to the utterly bewildered.' (Al Capp.)

'A fallen souffle is just a risen omelette. It depends on how you look at it, that's all, from above or below.' (Rabbi Lionel Blue.)

Back to practicalities and the bath. I must confess that I am more than a little disappointed with it. Although it is a magnificently stylish object of beauty, it has a mind of its own and is surprisingly hard to negotiate. It has been suggested that in order to avoid the tidal wave, I only half fill it before getting in. Unfortunately, that idea didn't work out too well. The bath has two gold taps – not at the end – but in the middle on the side. This is an awful feature which results in my top half being in the Arctic with my boobs resembling some sort of floating icebergs, while my poor legs are like overcooked lobsters. If I only half fill the bath before getting in, I then have to furiously paddle with my hands in order to circulate the water and make it even and I end up with the tidal wave effect yet again.

You might laugh, but this is all very upsetting for me because I hate showers and, now I'm getting older, I find it so hard to do the handstands in order to rinse off the private parts! Also, bath time has always been my time for 'thinking', which means that I don't seem to think so much these days and people might start judging me as a featherhead. What do I miss about the UK? My old bath!

In Cathedral Square in Christchurch we have a wizard! A real one! He wears a complete wizard costume and stands on a box talking about all sorts of issues, mainly philosophical. He invites people to make comments – a bit like Speakers Corner in Hyde Park – but no-one ever gets the better of him. The reason for this is that he is a retired university lecturer who obviously has a brilliant brain. He drives a VW car that's been altered and welded together so that it has two fronts and no rear.

To see it on the road you don't really know which way he is going! I couldn't help wondering if he does!

NZ is a developing country and although we have many wonderful things, we are still a little behind. One of the big hotels in Christchurch is called The Crown Plaza. The Crown Plaza has recently had a glass lift installed and this, of course, became a real talking point amongst the locals. Apparently, it was not unusual to see groups of grown businessmen with wide grins on their faces riding up and down. This became such a regular occurrence, the hotel management had a notice printed that said the lift was only to be used by the residents and was not for dinner guests!

'One out of four people in this country is mentally unbalanced. Think of your three closest friends; if they seem OK, then you're the one.' (Ann Landers.)

'Real friends are those who, when you've made a fool of yourself, don't think you've done a permanent job.' (Abraham Lincoln.)

I'm finding it hard to think of things I miss about the UK, apart from my friends, but I do miss the truly splendid ancient buildings and castles. Being such a young country, we have nothing like that here. Regardless of that, I have to tell you that everyday, as I drive along the coastline and look out at the sea and surf and then up to the magnificent mountains, topped with snow and set in a beautiful blue sky, I ask myself, 'What do you want to see a few old bricks for when you can see all this?'

We have just had a NZ version of *Test the Nation* here. I did the quiz and got 100% in the arts and history section, but failed miserably in politics and sports. It brought to mind a quote that I read ages ago when entertainment critics actually meant something to me: 'You know who critics are? The men who have failed in literature and art.' (Benjamin Disraeli.)

So, perhaps I should try for a job on the local paper as a critic, reviewing all the entertainment in Christchurch.

We Poms are known for whinging so here we go! Although this country is all pure and wonderful, I am amazed at all the junk mail that is delivered. It fills the post box every day! I just put it straight in the recycling bin, but not before I have checked it, because so many firms actually put biros or notepads in with their advertising stuff, so I'm jolly glad of that. I haven't bought a pen since I've been here!

Another whinge – the one meat I simply hate is lamb! Need I say more? Apart from not liking their most popular meat, I also don't like their dairy foods – milk, butter, cream – anything like that has a peculiar smell to it. So I decided to become a vegetarian, even to the point of having soy milk. I only did it for about a week because it had a funny and most embarrassing effect on me. I won't tell you all the details!

Andrew's mother and father came to dinner one night and I was saying how I'm still a little nervous of being totally alone. His dad told me of an idea that another lady living alone had – she simply put a pair of men's boots by the door, to give the impression that there was a man in the house. This seemed like a good idea to me and Andrew was quick to oblige with some old boots. The next time his dad visited, he also brought along an old pair of boots. Then the builders who are doing some work for me sorted out some more. It wasn't long before I had quite a collection on both the front and back door step. In fact, one of the builders wanted to swap his for Andrew's pair, which still had quite a bit of wear in them! I found all this very amusing until one of Jan's friends remarked that all those boots made it look as though I was running a house of ill-repute!

9

It is July, the equivalent of January in the UK. Of course it is chilly, but nothing like a British winter. The best thing of all is the garden. I have discovered that two of the trees are camelias and they are covered in gorgeous pink blossoms, so are japonicas and other trees that usually blossom in April or May in the UK. The locals have a blossom festival next month. Jan told me it takes ages to get adjusted to the fact that everything is the other way round.

What do I still miss about the UK? This time I'm going to say boot fairs. Sue and I used to love to wander around the boot fairs looking at other people's old treasures and I'm surprised the idea hasn't taken off here. Instead, they have garage sales. I haven't been to one, but it would be very embarrassing if you really didn't want to buy any of their junk! I think the boot fairs in fields are far more interesting and I quite miss them.

I really miss all my friends and the wonderful British sense of humour, so I wish the distance between us was only the Continent (say the distance between UK and Italy) because I would be able to pop back and visit Kent more frequently. Much to Jan's annoyance I often say to her; 'If only you had met Italian backpacker ... we'd all be Italy now!'

Sometimes, when I'm feeling a bit low, I look at the globe hanging from my ceiling just to check that I really am on the other side of the world, as far away as can be from the UK. Then of course the water-works start. I wish Colin was here – I miss him more than anything.

The hanging globe is made of plastic and one has to inflate it like a balloon. When I was clearing out Colin's study back home, one of my grandsons unexpectedly called in and saw how upset I was. He looked up at the globe and said, 'Granny, do you realise that you have something of Grandad here?' I agreed, I had a lot of things that belonged to Grandad, but he continued, 'No Granny, I mean something of his body. Look – his breath in that globe.' You can imagine how it shocked me to hear that and, of course, I resolved to always treasure the globe. When the time came to pack everything away in preparation for the big move, I bought a huge box, lined it with protective layers and lovingly placed it safely inside in preparation for the long journey to the other side of the world. Thankfully, it survived and is still here with me, hanging just above the computer and is one of my most treasured possessions.

I'm not sure I should admit to this because it seems to be rather morbid, but I feel overwhelmingly sad that I scattered Colin's ashes in England. At the time of doing so, I had no idea of the move that was in store for me. I really regret not having them here with me. In spite of that loss, I have tried to keep his memory alive by dedicating the whole of a bookcase in the sitting room to him, photographs and memorabilia of the various stages of his life. That way, not only are the family constantly reminded of him, but new friends coming into the house will know him too. Sometimes I long to 'get over it', to feel normal again – yet the paradox is that I can't let go and somehow I don't want to. I'm still shocked that I had no idea just how painful bereavement can be. If I had known, I certainly would have been far more caring to others suffering from the same condition in the past. It truly is hard to know what to do for the best when this happens. For example, I crave kindness and yet, when someone shows it with a gentle hug, instead of bringing comfort, it brings further despair. Will I ever feel better?

At least the garden has been shaping up reasonably well recently.

Although it is completely overgrown, I am looking forward to creating something pleasing. The first task was to clear out all the old debris and, since I really didn't feel up to it, I engaged a couple of gardeners to do the work for me. It actually took them three days to complete the job so I was glad I didn't even attempt it myself.

Next was to have a couple of patios built. Since the garden is so big, I thought they would enhance it. That was a completely extravagant thing to do, as there are already three other patio areas, a big deck and a courtyard, but there is a huge tree simply crying out for a circular patio surrounding it which I thought would give one the option of following the sun, or in my case, shade, and sit accordingly.

With regard to the layout, I decided to create an elegant Italian garden, mainly conifers of various size, colour and texture, plus a few suitable flowers, but only in white. Every time I ventured out, I seemed to be drawn to the garden centres and so it became a regular occurrence to struggle home with a car full of luscious plants tickling, spiking and often blinding me with their leaves.

Since our garden in England was similar to what I have planned here, I am already equipped with a copy of the statue of *The Bather* by Falconet rising from her bath, a statue depicting Cleopatra posing in a rather elegant fashion, a cherub bird bath and several large urns for plants. Although I was pleased to see old friends strategically placed amongst the foliage, there were a few gaps that I felt needed filling, so I set about finding other artistic pieces. This gave me tremendous pleasure.

It wasn't long before I had found a delightful chubby little cherub, leaning forward with one hand raised in a sort of 'blessing' pose. I sat him on a waist-high tree stump covered with trailing ivy and named him Raffaello.

Next was a dovecote, which seems to me to be reminiscent of more elegant Edwardian times. I must confess that I don't intend to keep any doves, not at present anyway, but I found a couple of stone doves, which don't look too crass at a distance and on a dark night. Lastly, a magnificent bust of Apollo on a column!

Apollo was a Greek God, not Roman, but since the early Romans also held him in high esteem and worshipped him, I have allowed him in. Apollo (like Colin) was a physician and apparently the Hippocratic Oath was based on Apollo's belief that 'life is sacred'. Everyone consulted with Apollo and he is known to have delivered deeply obscure responses – also like Colin! In his wisdom, he has inspired many sayings, such as 'Know thyself'; 'Speak well of the dead' and 'Nothing in excess'. With all this so similar to Colin, naturally I was pleased to give him a place in the garden. He also has a very gracious face and is actually very pleasing to the eye.

I have bought a garden bench and had a memorial plaque engraved for it, as one would for a grave, in remembrance of Colin. Now here is an odd story. Colin really loved the plant Soloman's Seal, so you will understand my surprise when it suddenly appeared right opposite the bench, just where he would be sitting if he were still here in body, enjoying it's beauty.

Another addition that I am very pleased with is my recycled Victorian claw foot bath. Being so old, even after resurfacing cracks started to reappear and since I really couldn't face going through all the inconvenience of sending it away again, I decided to get a brand new modern version fashioned in the same style. Now I have my precious old bath in the front garden planted with tiny white ivy geraniums, which I imagine might suggest bubbles, and I'm delighted to say that everyone who sees it remarks how extraordinary it looks.

The garden is beginning to give me a vague sense of satisfaction and I quite enjoy spending time tending it. Isn't there some saying about being close to God in the garden? In a strange way, I feel close to Colin too when I'm working in the garden and I feel sure he would approve of all that I am doing. If he were sitting on his memorial bench, under the pergola with the blooms of white clematis creeping overhead, looking at his favoured plants and the beautiful form of *The Bather* rising from her bath with the sun gently sinking in the sky, I'm sure his bow tie would be revolving in ecstasy.

I am getting a great deal of pleasure from my efforts, but I had a shock the other day – a rather pleasant shock! I found a male peacock strutting around the garden at the front, showing off his magnificent plumage. I thought what a wonderful accessory he would make in my gracious garden and felt tempted to rush and get a hammer and nails in order to tack his feet to the grass. Unfortunately, the downside with peacocks is the dreadful squawk they make, so perhaps I will shelve that idea.

Although I have been really busy of late, I did manage to get out and attend a Trafalgar Dinner at the Christchurch Club. It was a grand occasion with all the gentlemen in their naval, army or air force dress suits or normal evening dress, and, of course, medals were on full display. The ladies were in flowing evening dresses. I must confess that as I looked around at the exulted gathering, I couldn't help but be reminded of *The Muppets*! I wonder if you recall the two old boys who used to sit in the box at the theatre? I'll say no more.

'Don't talk to me about naval tradition. It's nothing but rum, sodomy, and the lash.' (Winston Churchill.)

'Stick close to your desks and never go sea, and you all may be rulers of the Queen's Navee!' (W.S. Gilbert.)

I thought of Colin and how he had never seemed to look that old and doddery. Colin was always young at heart and very pleasing to the eye and I'm so glad I have wonderful memories of him.

They were all very friendly and I was able to pass a very pleasant evening. I, of course, looked stunning! I've got to tell myself that now I haven't got a companion with excellent taste to do so!

I'm still struggling with the pain of his loss and, although I don't actually feel lonely, I sometimes feel so utterly alone. There is a subtle difference. I often reflect on these points and wonder if everyone else feels the same way. I think loneliness in someone often goes unnoticed because it can be hidden. You go out and about, meet people and chat to them, even develop friendships and generally join in with society and everyone accepts what they see in you – they might even be thinking you are coping well, but the fact still remains that you feel so very alone inside.

A LEAP INTO THE UNKNOWN

'If tears could build a stairway and memories a lane, I'd walk right up to Heaven and bring you home again'. (Unknown.) He is still constantly in my thoughts.

Now I have something awful to confess – the police have caught up with me and I have been fined for speeding! I find it so very hard to keep within the limit of 30 mph which is so strictly observed in NZ, and with my previous experience of driving an MG sports car, I readily admit to being a bit of a speed ace. Another thing in my defence is that the automatic car I now drive doesn't seem to help much, since I can feel it urging me to go faster. After paying up, I resolved to become more aware of the situation by sticking 'speed' signs at strategic places across the dashboard, as a reminder.

It occurred to me that the music I was playing wasn't conducive to sedate driving. Rachmaninov concertos just seemed to cause my foot to increase pressure on the accelerator. I tried Elgar, he being a respectable Edwardian English gentleman, but even he had moments of abandonment which caused me to become aroused, especially when I played all of his patriotic 'Land of Hope and Glory'! After much thought, I decided to play only gentle pastoral tunes, which I thought were much more suitable. That too proved to become rather exciting when it reached the spring section with all the little lambs joyously gambolling. Eventually, I realised that only nocturnes, adagios, largos etc. would help me in my effort to slow down. Now I drive, or should I say float, to the strains of the 'Barcarolle' by Offenbach, 'Canon in D' by Pachelbel and the likes, and the incredible thing is that I actually feel calmer and enjoy the ride more. So my advice to all you speed aces is to make a tape of suitably sedate music and watch out for those nasty cameras that tend to lurk in unexpected places. At my age, I don't know whether to be pleased or ashamed with myself for speeding.

When I arrived in NZ, I was horrified to learn that I had to take a theory test before I could be issued with a NZ driving licence and that I was only allowed to use my UK licence for a year. You have a book of 100 questions and answers that you need to learn. When you actually take the test, you have thirty-five questions picked at random and have to get thirty-two correct in order to pass – leaving you only three to get wrong so you really need to know all the answers! It's been years since I have taken any sort of examination and as the months were slipping away, I was becoming really nervous at the mere thought of it.

One morning, I woke at 4 a.m. and couldn't get back to sleep. By 4.30 a.m. I decided that this was the day I would take the test! I got up and sat at my desk for a couple of hours, going through the test book over and over again. By 8.30 a.m. I was standing outside the test centre, with a very wobbly tummy, ready to do the wretched thing. It was held in an AA building. When they opened, I went up to the desk and said I was here, raring to go. The lady, who was very laid back, first asked me to fill in a form – then take an eye test – then have my photograph taken – then pay the fee. By that time, imagine how nervous I was feeling, I just wanted to get on with it, but then she started to ask me if I belonged to the AA and to tell me all the advantages of doing so. I could stand the delay no longer, so I had to say to her, very politely of course, that I just couldn't take it all in at the moment since my mind was focused on the test! How insensitive these people can be. I was feeling really miffed with her and slightly thrown off course.

Eventually I got the paper and was shown to a booth. A little later, when I emerged, I had a very broad grin on my face and I just couldn't control it. You know how you are doing as you progress because each question has an option of three answers and you have to simply scratch what you think is the correct answer, after which you see either a cross or a tick, therefore I knew that I had got 100% correct. I was so relieved and overjoyed and just couldn't stop smiling. I only wished I had someone with me so that we could hug each other and jump around the room like Colin and I did whenever something wonderful had happened. I arrived at the desk and she, being the insensitive receptionist, took the paper, checked it and, without even looking my way, started to process it. I felt so deflated that I couldn't resist asking if she had noticed my 100% and to tell her that I was expecting a virile young man to jump out from behind the desk, waving a wad of $75,000 in one hand and a bottle of champagne in the other and congratulate me for being the first ever person intelligent enough to get full marks (let me repeat here) 100%! Do you know what she said to me? 'We don't do that here.' That's NZ for you; they simply don't have the English sense of humour. All that was left for me to do was drive home and telephone Jan and Sue to tell them the results and, I must say, they were so surprised that it left me with the feeling that they thought I was so much of a featherhead, I couldn't possibly have done it.

Back in the UK, the shop I mostly frequented was Marks and Spencer! Here it is a place called Bunnings, a large hardware store, similar to B&Q only on a far bigger scale. The reason for this is that I am still doing odd jobs around the house and garden. The last time I visited there I noticed something that I thought was really wonderful. They had a big notice about DIY lessons for children at the weekends. Don't you think that's a good idea? I was really impressed and I expect the kids love it. I only wish I could have joined because I now realise that there is nearly always something that needs repairing – how I miss Colin.

I paid a wonderful visit to my friends in Sydney. When I arrived they were there ready to meet me and take me back to their apartment, where they served me a champagne breakfast. All very nice, but I had had the very same on the plane on the way over. Of course, I didn't want to disappoint them, so I forced myself to consume more and so by the time I arrived at the hotel, I was ready to tumble into bed.

I am beginning to understand just how very big the world is. Trips from the UK across to the Continent now seem so insignificant. Although I understood the various time zones flying around the world – say from the UK to NZ – I was quite surprised to find that Australia has a different time from NZ. After all, they look so close together on the map!

We Brits tend to think that London is marvellous, and so it is, but I was amazed at Sydney. I should think it must be one of the world's premier locations. It is quite overwhelming!

Here is a little of its history; in April 1770, Captain Cook landed at Botany Bay, Sydney, claiming the entire east coast of Australia for Britain and by 1788, convicts, soldiers and a handful of settlers established a remote new colony. Since that time, Sydney now has a population of more than 4 million people of over 200 nationalities, speaking 20 different languages! You can clearly see the early influence from British landmarks such as Hyde Park, King's Cross, Piccadilly, The Strand etc.

Sydney encompasses a great variety of precincts and districts and is a mecca for shopping – but the harbour area is particularly interesting and it was very exciting for me to actually see the world famous Opera House. In spite of the glass and concrete jungle of high-rise buildings surrounding the harbour, it also has many small sandy bays and it's just as easy to enjoy a dip as it is to shop. I suppose the most well known of all these is Bondi Beach. Golden sands, surf, sun and beautifully clear water are never far away.

Naturally, there are plenty of cruise ships in and out, a ferry to the surrounding beaches and also plenty of harbour cruises for the visitors. I must confess to being totally stunned as I flew into Sydney airport. I just didn't realise how very big it would be and I hadn't seen such high sky scrapers before, except in Kuala Lumpur. It all seemed to be straight out of a James Bond movie!

The hotel where I was booked to stay was directly at the water's edge and my room had a balcony. One morning, I was quietly sitting watching the surfers, when a huge white crested cockatoo landed and strutted up and down, keeping his beady eye on me and squawking! It was quite alarming; I was told the visitors often feed them, so that's what they expect. Another time, I was reading a book and, out of the corner of my eye, I could see movement. On closer inspection it turned out to be a gecko, a small lizard.

One day, walking around town with the temperature well into the seventies, a Father Christmas in all his furs passed by, ringing a bell, advertising a newly opened Christmas shop. It all seemed so incongruous. I know I will always miss Christmas in the UK.

I must say, everything is pretty amazing in Sydney, but for me the highlight was going to see Puccini's *La Boheme* at the Opera House. Imagine how I felt sipping cocktails in such a grand place, overlooking all the lights of the harbour. I only wish Colin could have been there and I must confess to feeling a little guilty at enjoying such a spectacular evening.

One thing that really pleased and surprised me was that when the plane was coming into land at Christchurch airport I had a real feeling of 'coming home'. It seems that I have totally adopted this new country as my own.

Woe is me – what misery! After all I've had to have done to the house, the straw that broke the camel's back has happened and I'm beginning to feel somewhat sorry for myself. As you know, I've had a procession of gentlemen in, one after another, to do various work for me and although they have mostly been young, handsome and virile with rippling muscles, it has been of little comfort to me. Which, of course, proves yet another disappointing thing. My lack of interest in them firmly establishes the fact that I am over the hill, past my sell by date and only fit to be put out to graze!

Anyway, the final job was to have new lino throughout a downstairs bathroom, laundry and kitchen. Naturally, all electrical appliances had to be removed, so out came the fridge freezer, the washing machine and the dishwasher. (Why isn't anything easy?) The young men set about ripping up the old lino. I could see that it was a real effort and it wasn't going too well. Several glasses jumped off the kitchen shelves, smashing to the floor with the vibration of their equipment and dust was falling everywhere, settling like snow on every surrounding surface – but worse was to come. They accidentally smashed the entire base of the lavatory pedestal! I felt so sorry for them, because they too were horrified. This led to various phone calls and I now have to postpone the actual laying of the lino, go and choose a new bathroom set, get the builder to collect and deliver it, get a plumber to install it and then get the lino people back again. In the meantime I am left with the fridge freezer in the sitting room and the rest of the appliances lying idle in the garage.

I must say, the Flanders and Swann song 'The Gasman Cometh'

came to mind. 'Twas on a Monday morning the gas man came to call' – it then goes on to say how each tradesman caused an accident which lead to another tradesman calling in each day and concluding the song with; 'It all makes work for the working man to do!' The NZ working man has had plenty to do at my expense!

Just to prove just how involved the whole procedure was, here is a brief account of it:

1. All electrical appliances are removed from the kitchen in preparation;
2. The gentlemen come to remove the old lino;
3. In the process, the lavatory pedestal is smashed;
4. The lino cannot be fitted until the lavatory is replaced;
5. I wait, without the use of the kitchen stuff for one week for the loo to be delivered;
6. The loo comes and I arrange for the lino to be laid;
7. Two days later, the lino arrives with a flaw running all the way through it;
8. I wait a further week for more lino. Still no kitchen appliances in situ;
9. The lino arrives. When unrolled, it is the wrong design;
10. I have a well overdue nervous breakdown and, in desperation, decide to have the pattern that has been sent;
11. The gentleman who is laying it informs me that, due to the pattern change, there isn't enough to fit the area;
12. I ring the shop and, after an afternoon of to-ing and fro-ing, more lino is eventually delivered;
13. Yippee! The lino is at last down;
14. I now need the plumber to install the appliances that were taken out;
15. Four days later the plumber comes;
16. Two hours later my friends from Alexandra arrive to stay!

Unfortunately the difference in size of the new toilet and shower unit that have been fitted has left me with large unpainted spaces on the wall, which in turn means that I will have to have the entire room redecorated!

A LEAP INTO THE UNKNOWN

Now for a little scenario involving the lino man and me:

Me. I wonder if you can help me before you go?
He. Of course.
Me. You see, it's so difficult without a man in the house.
He. Of course, I'll try.
Me. Thanks – it's very much appreciated.
He. It's harder that I thought. Can you help?
Me. OK, I'll try. It will be so nice to have it in place again.
He. I'll push hard and you try to guide me.
Me. Take it slowly, it's a bit too big for me and I don't want the floor marked.
He. Let's try sliding it in.
Me. Nearly there. Keep pushing.
He. It's so big I just can't see where I'm going.
Me. Keep going, it's ready to go in. Stop! I'm stuck.
He. Try to squeeze out.
Me. I can't move.
He. I'll try to back out a bit.
Me. Oh, that's better.
He. Can you get the plug in?
Me. No, I can't reach it.
He. Can't you stretch a little?
Me. Got it. OK. I'll try to get out.
He. Here we go – got it – nearly there – it's in. I thought for a minute I would have to send for assistance.
Me. Thanks, so much, it's so good to have everything in working order again.
He. You're welcome. It's been a pleasure!

Regardless of what you may think, that was the two of us trying to move the enormous fridge freezer out of the sitting room into a custom-made space for it in the kitchen.

Back to the subject of weather. A really odd thing happened the other day, even the locals were alarmed. It is springtime here and everyone is in shorts and T-shirts, but we had two days of blizzards, enormous hail stones, torrential rain, severe winds and ... snow. Unheard of in this part of NZ, except for on the very tops of the mountains. Anyway, it brought Christchurch to a standstill. Being sports orientated, they were out in their skiing gear, actually skiing down the streets of Christchurch! They can be completely mad sometimes. Two days later all the snow was gone, the sun shining and people were back in shorts and T-shirts!

10

I had a lovely surprise the other day. A lady phoned me quite out of the blue and said she had heard of me and would I like to go to yoga with her (don't laugh) and also to a club called the U3A (University of the Third Age). I was rather reticent to try the yoga, and I was even more horrified on meeting her to find that she is a retired PE teacher and has the typical 'jolly hockey sticks' attitude to sport. However, I explained that I hated sweating and avoided any physical activities but she was very sweet about it and assured me I would soon come to love it. Of course, in order to make a friend one has to be sociably agreeable to kind invitations, so with great trepidation, I went along for the torture.

What a surprise I had! The instructor was a lady of eighty-four, the rest of the class consisted of seventy, eighty and even ninety-year olds and I was the spring chicken! But more surprise was in store. While I was practically stuck on each movement, hardly able to move, these old girls were performing the most complicated contortions with great ease, swinging their arms and legs all over the place. The only huffing and puffing was coming from my mat.

It certainly opened my eyes as to how unfit I must be, so I have decided to continue these lessons until I can at least touch my toes instead of having my hands dangling only in my knee region! They appeared to be real 'ladies' of Sumner, very pleasant and welcoming, so I shall enjoy their company.

The very next day I went with her and her husband to a U3A meeting and thoroughly enjoyed it. I am delighted with that introduction. The U3A is a movement that is basically an academic learning community for retired people, with retired lecturers sharing their experiences and knowledge. 'The Third Age' comes from a definition of a typical lifespan into three ages (stages), which may loosely be described as the first age being that of childhood and youthful dependence, leading to the second age of independence, maturity, home building and work, leading to the third age of active retirement.

I am reminded of Shakespeare's 'All the world's a stage' monologue from *As You Like It*:

> All the world's a stage,
> And all the men and women merely players:
> They have their exits and their entrances;
> And one man in his time plays many parts,
> His acts being seven ages. As, first the infant,
> Mewling and puking in the nurse's-arms.
> Then the whining school-boy, with his satchel
> And shining morning face, creeping like snail
> Unwillingly to school. And then the lover,
> Sighing like furnace, with a woeful ballad
> Made to his mistress' eyebrow. Then the soldier,
> Full of strange oaths and bearded like the bard
> Jealous in honour, sudden and quick in quarrel,
> Seeking the bubble reputation
> Even in the cannon's mouth. And then the justice,
> In fair round belly with good capon lined,
> With eyes severe and beard of formal cut,
> Full of wise saws and modern instances,
> And so he plays his part. The sixth age shifts
> Into the lean and slipper'd pantaloon

> With spectacles on nose and pouch on side,
> His youthful hose, well saved, a world too wide
> For his shrunk shank, and his big manly voice,
> Turning again toward childish treble, pipes
> And whistles in his sound. Last scene of all,
> That ends this strange eventful history,
> Is second childishness, and mere oblivion,
> Sans teeth, sans eyes, sans taste, sans everything.

This group is just the sort of thing I know I will enjoy because it is learning for pleasure with none of the trauma of facing exams! Apart from the monthly general meeting, there are other groups focusing on various subjects such as books and writing, art, music appreciation and theatre which also meet each month.

I am really overjoyed about all this because, apart from doing the studying, which I love, another couple have befriended me and I have many social events to attend.

My British friends Alfred and Barbara have invited me to join them on a visit to Norfolk Island, so after all the problems restoring the house, I thought I would treat myself to a little holiday. Norfolk is New Zealand's closest neighbour (approximately a two-hour flight away) and retains the magical remoteness which, over a century ago, attracted the intrepid descendants of the Bounty mutiny as well as convicts and bandits, who have all had their place there since its discovery in 1774. After discovering and naming the island, Captain James Cook wrote; 'This is an island paradise.'

The locals say it is a place for 'newly-weds or nearly-deads' because all that Norfolk Island has to offer is beauty, tranquillity, a subtropical climate, history and the simple things in life. A history buff would be in his element here, as was I. You do not just see the penal settlement and artefacts, you can actually 'feel' them. It is reputed to be haunted by many ghosts.

The story is that a ship under Captain Bligh's command was sailing to Tahiti. Bligh was renowned for being a harsh and cruel captain; during the journey there was a mutiny lead by Fletcher

Christian. Four of the mutineers landed on the island and settled there. There were only fifteen women living on the island but the men started families and built homes. The interesting thing is that there are still only one hundred and seventy-five inhabitants on the island and they all can trace their ancestors back to the original four sailors who were named Christian, Adams, Buffet and Quintal – and still bear their names. Because it is so remote, when the British were sending convicts to Australia, they sent the very worst to Norfolk Island.

Not only is the island remote, it is also tiny – around four and a half miles one way by two and a half miles the other! To walk around in the church-like silence, treading beneath towering trunks of mighty Norfolk pines on a thick carpet of dropped pine leaves is awe-inspiring. Add to this the beauty of luscious hibiscus flowers growing in abundance everywhere and you feel quite overwhelmed. Visitors can play golf and go fishing, diving and snorkeling, bushwalking, horse riding and mountain biking. There are also the customary club activities of bridge, bowls, chess, tennis, squash etc.

Because the islanders rely on the tourist trade, they have social activities available every evening. I went to a Tahitian dance night – really lovely, up on a cliff top with maidens dressed in Tahitian costumes of grass skirts, neck garlands and flowers in their hair, followed by food and wine. I managed to keep quiet and sit tight on that evening but I soon got caught out. The next evening I went to a Tahitian evening of a different kind, where all the guests (the tourists) had to take part in a dramatised history of the inhabitants. I was given the part of a 'spinster' so I heaved a sigh of relief, thinking that I would escape by sitting out much of the time in this sedentary role. After all, what could an old spinster possibly have to act out? I soon found out! Much to my surprise, the spinster was a sexpot and an experienced dancer! I must say, I was filled with horror because I had to stand up and be taught how to sway my hips while gently waving my arms around – all this in front of the audience! As it happens, I am very limited in that department since you can't get much action out of a hip replacement and an arm that is stiff due to a fractured shoulder.

Nevertheless, I did my best and was pleasantly surprised at what I managed to achieve. Another evening there was an enactment of the mutiny on the Bounty – incorporating a murder mystery. The locals must have such a laugh about it all because they arrange the evening entertainments, give everyone a costume to wear and a script, then sit back and watch the tourists pay for the privilege of performing the entertainment themselves!

Something that rather amused me was that Warren, the gentleman who was originally the driver of the coach from the airport, then turned into a courier telling us all the history of the island – the next time we saw him he was part of the Tahitian dance evening. On another occasion we went to a dramatisation of the settlers arriving, we the tourists being the settlers and he playing the governor, greeting us with welcoming drinks. On yet another occasion, we had to attend church to give thanks for a safe journey and he played the parson and took the service. I later asked him if he had a 'real' job, to which he replied that he was the gravedigger – and with the inhabitants numbering merely 175, I soon deduced that he had very little work to do! I think one of the funniest things I will remember is that on boarding the coach to go home, I glanced out to see Warren in fits of laughter, just peeking over the wall. I was reminded of this anonymous piece of prose, which I thought was rather apt:

> Once upon a time there were four people – Everybody, Somebody, Nobody and Anybody. When there was an important job to be done, Everybody was sure Somebody would do it. Anybody could have done it but Nobody did it. When Nobody did it, Everybody got angry because it was Somebody's job. Everybody thought that Somebody would do it, but Nobody realised that Nobody would do it. So it ended up that Everybody blamed Somebody when Nobody did what Anybody could have done in the first place.

And my comment – thank God that Norfolk Island has Warren! I flew up to Wellington for Sue's birthday and spent a week with the family. Wellington is a very impressive city, similar to Sydney. One day we went into town to visit their big department store, which to my surprise is nearly as big as Harrods. They had a Christmas shop on the top floor so Sue and I decided we would go to see exactly how the New Zealanders decorated their homes, quite expecting that since Christmas is in the sun, it would amount to practically nothing. Were we surprised? It was absolutely fabulous.

I counted thirty-two 'themed' Christmas trees all adorned in appropriate decorations. Apart from the customary gold, silver or white snowflakes, there was an Eastern tree covered in caskets of jewels; a gingerbread man tree; a candy tree full of sticks of rock; a tree depicting the holy family; a snowman tree; a baby tree, all pink and blue bottles, rattles and such; a musical instrument tree; a pets' tree with little dogs and cats; a clown's tree which was very colourful; a totally red tree; a Father Christmas tree; an ABC tree; an elves and fairies tree; a toy soldier tree; a theatrical tree, full of all sorts of interesting stuff. And now getting to the most original – a teenage girl's tree with lipstick, handbags etc. all made of glittery stuff, and an old lady's tree, which was hilarious. It had the same sort of stuff as the teenage tree, only the handbags and shoes were styled to suit the age, and the old ladies were all in pink either standing, sitting or reclining seductively on chairs or sofas. They had very large tummies!

Another rather interesting tree was seaside-themed with fat ladies and gentlemen in old-fashioned swimsuits with rubber rings, boats and ice-cream. That appealed to me especially since both Sue and I now live at the seaside.

But my favourite of all was a thoroughly outrageous tree – which I can only describe as a tart's tree! It too had handbags and shoes but everything was way over the top in bright red and mauve feathers etc. What really amused me was the fact that there were matching tart's stockings to hang on the fireplace, but not made of the usual Father Christmas material – they were made of sexy fishnet stocking material with a garter at the top and a high heel shoe at the bottom.

Truly it was all so fabulous I'm not sure if I've done it justice. I've never seen anything like it before and was utterly spellbound by it all.

Now that summer is here, I am observing things that I seemed to have missed when I first arrived. For example, the changing of the seasons and how the locals protect their children. Obviously, I still haven't registered the importance of the sun's rays in spite of the fact that I have already been seriously burned. It must be the rule that all children go to school in the most peculiar wide-brimmed sunhats and continue to wear them in the playground. I must say, it looks rather odd to see little people with such large hats, nevertheless they seem to accept it as normal. Apparently, when they arrive at school, one of the first things the teacher does is to hand out the suntan protection to everyone. I now know for sure I'll be far more careful than when I first came and suffered dreadfully from sunburn.

Another interesting thing about the school children is the fact that they are their own lollipop people. Outside every school are two enormous orange lollipops, either side of the road, mounted on a bracket. The children on duty swing them around into the road in order to stop the traffic when others are gathered to cross safely.

I've also noticed that there are certain items that every adult seems to carry. Everyone wears sunglasses and even if the sun isn't shining, they walk around with them perched on the top of their heads – summer or winter. And everyone is clutching a bottle of water. This is something that I have automatically adopted since the air is so dry, one needs to be constantly sipping water for refreshment.

The two seagulls nesting only metres away from a busy causeway are back again this year. It is believed they are the same pair and, as last season, a barrier has been erected with a large notice 'Wildlife – Protected Area'. They certainly know how to choose their location; fabulous sea views and close to amenities, with the added attraction of an adoring public. Actually, I think it is rather dangerous to let them stay there because one can't help 'rubber necking' when driving past. Today I saw two fluffy little chicks which was an absolute delight, but I have no doubt that someone is going to run into the back of another car before long!

I have just had a wonderful visit from friends Tom and Elizabeth from the UK. They were here for three weeks and it all went really well because Tom actually likes cooking(!) and took great pleasure in planning our meals. My contribution was to be chauffeur and in doing so, I saw so much more of the area and also gained tremendous confidence in tackling the mountains and other difficult roads. I think I could cope with a jumbo jet now. The summits are amazing, not only exceedingly high, but twisting and turning and quite scary at first, but both Elizabeth and Tom assured me that I drove well and that they had every confidence in me. I omitted to tell them that I too was so scared, sometimes I had actually closed my eyes! Only joking.

Christmas is nearly here and I can hardly believe that this time last year I was homeless! Christmas will never be the same again for me and so I think I am in the best place here. The sun is shining and, although the locals seem to be getting in the swing of things, it all seems so incongruous to me that I've quite easily crossed the festive season off my list of things to do. I can't help but think of England and, although the pain of leaving seems to be fading, I still think of the good times that Colin and I had in our friends' company back home.

I've just had a wonderful day out with Jan. It was a Christmas country fête, held in the rural town of Culverden. The whole day was an absolute delight. The area is so beautiful – rolling hills, interesting rock formations, blue skies and sheep grazing. There were stalls selling all sorts of unusual goodies, cookery demonstrations, live music and much more. There was also wine tasting, very popular in this region of NZ. I must confess to forcing myself to sample just a few. They even had some very civilised Pimms so I spent a pleasant interlude sitting on bales of straw under the shade of a tree, serenaded by live music. I seemed to get stuck on the bales of straw with the food and drink and since the weather has now settled into hot, balmy days, it was a very pleasant experience.

'Sometimes when I reflect back on all the wine I drink, I feel shame. Then I look into the glass and think about the workers in the vineyards and all of their hopes and dreams. If I didn't drink this wine, they might be out of work and their dreams would be shattered. Then I say to myself, "It is better that I drink this wine and let their dreams come true than be selfish and worry about my liver".' (Jack Handey.)

A few days later, I had a real hair-raising experience. Jan wanted a horse truck in order to cart her horse around to the various trials. She eventually found one that she thought would be just right but, unfortunately, it was on the North Island, so we hatched a plan to fly up to Wellington, pick up the truck, take it on the ferry over to the South Island and finally drive it home to Sumner. So far, so good.

The flight, as ever, was good and I'm beginning to get accustomed to hopping on and off planes as we do with London buses. Sue picked us up from the airport and drove us to the ferry terminal, where we waited for the truck to be delivered. What a shock I had when it arrived. It was enormous! It had a huge cockpit with seating for three, which was so high off the ground that the girls had to push my bum up as I tried to get in and then practically lift me out when I needed it. Behind the cockpit is a kitchen area, which is going to be my domain – I've already started calling it the hospitality room. It has many wooden cupboards, a sink, a fridge and even a small settee. The main body of the truck is where the horses ride; there are stalls for two horses and space for all the paraphernalia.

This truck is big but with much crunching of the gears, swearing and cursing, we managed to do the one-hour ride from Wellington to Paraparaumu Beach, where Sue lives and where we intended to stay the night.

The next morning, we were up at the crack of dawn in order to get the 7.45 a.m. ferry over to the South Island, followed by the 6-hour drive to Christchurch and Sumner. The biggest hurdle was getting the vehicle on and off the ferry; the cockpit was so high that it was hard to judge exactly how close we were to other vehicles and, naturally, Jan was scared that she might have to perform some fancy driving and actually reverse it in order to get it parked in place. The noise of the engine was so great that, to be heard, we had to shout to each other. Thankfully, after much shouting and screaming, we managed to park it in position without scraping other vehicles or flattening helpful ferry workers. After that ordeal, we were glad to relax during the 4-hour ferry crossing.

Landing the other side, we continued our journey down the South Island reasonably well considering we had to negotiate driving up, down and around mountains, cross river bridges and such, all the while yelling our heads off at each other. I should mention here that the scenery was amazing. The road down to Christchurch is coastal in places and I could see beautiful sandy beaches and many seals sunning themselves on rocks. The wayside was ablaze with wild lupins and gorgeous huge white lilies, and we passed meadow after meadow of lush green grass with grazing sheep. In such an elevated position, I saw a lot more of the country than ever before in a car and we had a few laughs on the way. By the time we eventually arrived in Sumner, we were exhausted and both had the sorest of bottoms. Naturally, I was glad to be back in the sanctuary of my house, where I put my feet up and had a refreshing glass of chilled wine. It had been a real adventure.

I have started a new hobby – nothing too physical. I have started to learn bridge. It is very fashionable here, and a dear old lady told me that it would open many doors to me. Since the idea of going to the gym to make some friends fills me with horror, I've opted for bridge, which I find more appealing. I'm pleased to say that I really enjoyed the first lesson and feel quite confident I could develop into a reasonable player. I was on a table with ladies similar to myself in age and we rather gelled in our quest for some intellectual stimulation. Half way through there was a short interval where we were offered tea or coffee and since we all agreed we would rather have a gin and tonic, our friendship was well and truly sealed.

During the game of bridge, it is required that a person be 'dummy'. Being dummy means that your hand of cards is set out on the table for all to see and your partner not only plays their hand, but also yours. During this time, you simply sit out watching the game progress with no effort on your behalf. One of the ladies, when it was her turn to be dummy, announced in a very loud voice, 'Oh I simply love being dummy. May I always be dummy?' Which virtually meant that she wanted to be part of the bridge scene, but not actually be involved in the tricky activity of playing it!

This last week has been Cup Week, the NZ equivalent of Ascot. I could have gone with the Christchurch Club, but still had too much to do at home, so decided to give it a miss this year. Nevertheless I was interested to read a report in the paper by someone who described the trouble and care she went to in choosing an outfit and hat, but concluded, 'Unfortunately, I disgraced myself by being eventually carried out of the Lindauer (NZ sparkling wine) tent over the shoulder of a charming security bloke called Bruce, blissfully unaware that any horses had ever entered the arena.' What a hoot!

Eventually the exterior painters finished and the house looked immaculate. I was feeling very serene and happy. I had spent a very satisfying morning working in the garden and decided to reward myself with the delights of a bubble bath and perhaps a nice cool glass of bubbles. Although I live alone, it is really important to me to continue to wear make-up and dress smartly even though I may not be seen by anyone that day. I feel it's a matter of 'keeping my end up', whatever that means, so that's exactly what I did after the bath. Feeling rather grand and looking particularly stunning, I recharged my glass and drifted into the garden, surveying all in front of me with great satisfaction.

We had been having blistering hot sunny days, so I had been

watering the garden with three hose pipes with sprayers attached. There is an irrigation system installed which I hadn't used as yet, but as I floated down the garden, bubbles in hand and feeling very satisfied with myself, I noticed a little tap and thought I would save myself the trouble of manually watering, and give the irrigation system a try. I stooped to turn on the tap, totally unaware that, like everything else in this place, it was not working properly, and an almighty spurt of water gushed out all over the place, sending me reeling backwards, completely and utterly soaked. Soaked through to the skin with hair flattened to my head and water dripping off the end of my nose and, horror of horrors, the bubbles had even jumped out of the glass over my shoulder!

'You can only find out by trying.' (Greek proverb.)

'It's astonishing in this world how things don't turn out at all the way you expect them to.' (Agatha Christie.)

11

I have to confess to some awful things that I am beginning to do. I always paid attention to my appearance, as Granny taught me to, but things seem to be altering in that department. For example, I have persistently drifted around in my flowing skirts, only to find that apart from being somewhat impractical, people tend to look at me and wonder if I am an ageing hippy. I must own up to now possessing several pairs of shorts and feeling totally relaxed wearing them.

I also have to confess to owning a backpack. Knowing my love of handbags and the fact that I could open a shop with my collection, you must realise what a drastic change it has been for me, but it is truly wonderful and I really needed one! Honestly. Lip salve and 'sunnies' (as the New Zealanders call sunglasses) are essential at all times, but I now also carry a bottle of water. My backpack contains a fleece for cold snaps and a rain mac for showers – I don't bother with an umbrella, since the wind is so fierce, it would turn it inside out anyway. I carry a scarf to save the horses being scared when my wig flies off. Of course, I carry sun protection and also insect protection. I find I need a camera to record all the wonderful things I see and also a map so that I know where I am. I need to have identification, just in case something awful should befall me and no-one claims me! Naturally, I carry a photograph of Colin – well, who carries a photo of someone you see every day? And, of course, a purse for essentials. I carry tissues because they come in handy. As yet I haven't resorted to paper pants – I'm still all right in that department – but I do carry plasters because I tend to fall over quite frequently, and not due to booze I hasten to add! I can't think what else, but I must say my life has been enriched so much since I have had a backpack. The only things I haven't given up are my high-heels – oops – they must be why I need the identification and the plasters! Apart from all that, I'm still British! You might like to hold the thought of me in my shorts, backpack on my back, striding along singing, 'I love to go a-wandering, along the mountain track and, as I go, I love to sing, my knapsack on my back'!

I have a very interesting and wonderful tale to tell you to start the New Year. I was asked to give a talk to the Christchurch Club, and since I hadn't done any public speaking or singing since I left the UK, I wasn't feeling very confident about it. However, I thought I ought to do it, so dutifully went along, planning to speak about my experiences in teaching and entertainment. The first thing that filled me with horror was that I didn't have either Colin or my maid, who had both always helped me with costume changes etc. Bravely, I very slowly and carefully set up the PA system and then sat down to have dinner with the assembled guests. It was arranged that I would give my talk between the main course and the dessert.

Colin always used to ask me if I had checked my battery for the radio mike before I started talking. He asked this every single time, so you can understand my shock when I realised, just as I was about to go on, that the battery was completely dead. I simply hadn't used it since leaving England. Of course, it caused rather a commotion, which was resolved by the manager going out to find an all-night place that may possibly stock such a battery and the chef (and we all know how temperamental chefs can be) having to serve the sweet ahead of time!

Due to nerves, I developed verbal diarrhoea during the wait and felt compelled to tell all surrounding me how annoyed my husband would have been at such a thing. I said several times to various people how annoyed he would have been with me. I didn't use the word cross or mad – just annoyed! While we were all waiting for the batteries to arrive, the chairman came to me and started speaking and, I, of course, repeated that my husband would be so annoyed with me. During the dinner there had been the customary crackers and he picked up the last one and said, 'Here – cheer yourself up and pull this with me.' It contained the following joke:

Q. When does a doctor become annoyed?
A. When he is out of patients.

There must have been billions of crackers pulled all over the world that night, but the way I looked at it was that it was a connection with Colin. He really was with me.

'Tis strange – but true; for truth is always strange; stranger than fiction.' (Lord Byron.)

Now for my latest acquisition. Since the property is surrounded by trees and blossoms that need clearing and my shoulder injury hurts so much when I try to do such jobs, a garden hoover seemed the answer to my problems. I loved the idea of it, but it proved to be more than I could cope with because it seemed to have a mind of its own. All in good faith I would move in a certain direction, but the strength of the thing seemed to drag me somewhere entirely different, rendering me completely out of control. In fact, it felt like an elephant on steroids! I wasn't going to give in and felt determined to keep it under control, so I continued with the ongoing battle. As you use it the bag soon fills so you need to empty it occasionally and, unfortunately, that is where I came unstuck. I'm not that stupid that I don't know where all the stuff goes, but the first time I needed to empty it I felt rather in need of a practical man's help! I kept saying to myself, 'You can do it – you can do it,' and I felt sure I could, so slowly I proceeded to empty the bag, reassemble it and continue hoovering. I found that, for some strange reason, I was not only being dragged all over the place, but experiencing a strange overwhelming gust which was covering me with chewed up twigs and leaves and making my wig stand on end. On inspection, I discovered that I had forgotten to zip up the bag again and all the muck was being recirculated. I resembled some sort of Halloween character or a wicked witch in a pantomime! In my defence, I must say that surely I am becoming a little wiser because instead of cursing and swearing, I am beginning to look to my own stupidity. That's life – if you can't learn as you go along, where would you be?

12

The Coast to Coast race took place recently, a challenging test of physical skill and strength. The race is over two days, starting on the West Coast of NZ and ending right here in Sumner on the East Coast. Much to my amazement, this is what the contestants have to do:
1. Jump on a bike and cycle to a certain point (I'm not sure how many miles, but it must be a lot because west to east is many many miles);
2. Reaching the mountains, you proceed to run up and over. (A friend of Jan's did that part in five hours! Imagine that, running for five hours over a mountain!);
3. When you reach the other side of the mountain, your support team have your bike ready and you ride to a river;
4. Reaching the river, you jump in your kayak (I'm not sure of the distances) and paddle upstream for all you're worth;
5. More running and lastly cycling into the East Coast area, finishing at Sumner.

I feel weary just relaying this to you. Just imagine how very fit – and utterly mad – these young people must be!

Sumner was absolutely bursting with enthusiastic followers that weekend. There were cars, Camper vans, trailers with bikes and kayaks etc. and the atmosphere was buzzing with excitement. They sure are a mad lot, these New Zealanders!

Wes, one of my grandsons, came to stay for the week prior to the race and as we drove out one day, we saw a group of men practising on their bikes in preparation for it and, low and behold, they were all in fancy dress. I assume it must have been to raise money for charity – or beer! They were extremely amusing. There was Batman, a jail bird, someone in a Victorian nightshirt, and many others but the funniest of all was a great big fella with enormous thighs who was dressed as a saucy French maid. He was actually wearing frilly knickers, suspenders and black stockings and, with a huge expanse of white thigh at the top of his leg, it was even funnier to see him peddling like mad with the stocking tops flashing up and down.

Almost immediately after my English friends and my grandson Wesley left, more friends arrived from the UK. I was delighted and this time I was able to enjoy a little holiday myself, too. I flew up to Auckland to meet them and we hired a rental car and drove all the way down to Christchurch. Directly from the airport, our first overnight stop was the Coromandel Peninsula, an area renowned for its beautiful surf and swimming beaches. Unfortunately, we didn't take advantage of those since we had to press on to our next stop, Rotorua, which was of more interest to us. Rotorua has so very many attractions that we were spoilt for choice. We went on a 'duck tour', a ninety-minute scenic adventure on a WW2 landing craft that could travel along the roads and onto the lakes. They called it a duck tour because the craft was painted yellow and we were all issued with a sort of whistle which sounded just like a duck quacking! That immediately alerted me to silly capers, nevertheless every time we passed anybody we all had to blow our whistle to check whether they were locals or tourists. Locals looked the other way in disgust, while fellow tourists hooted with laughter!

The best touristy thing I have done so far was the 'Maori Experience'. It was absolutely wonderful. The Rotorua region is home to the Arawa people, who trace their ancestry back to the

A LEAP INTO THE UNKNOWN

Arawa canoe, believed to have sailed from the Polynesian homelands of Hawaiki. We all bundled onto a coach and were taken to their village. After an exceedingly warm greeting, we were taken outside to witness our dinner being prepared in the *hangi*, an earth oven. Heated stones and covered food are carefully put into a pit to cook. It really didn't look very inviting. We were then lead on a track through a densely wooded area, with a few shocks on the way because, here and there, we came upon Maori carvings of a rather scary nature. As we progressed deeper into the wood, we began to hear threatening calls from the Maoris and if you turned round to see where they were coming from, all you caught sight of was the back of a leg or something stirring in the bushes. It really conjured up a picture of the early settlers and the threat they must have felt on encounters with the Maori and the courage they must have had when they first landed in this country. The track we were walking along had a sheer drop at one side and there was a river running along the bottom. After a while, the chanting of the Maoris became louder and a *Te Toki-a-Tapiri* (war canoe) appeared with about a dozen warriors skillfully rowing and chanting. It really became quite alarming, but the spell was broken with they got out of the canoe on the other side of the river and it was all bare bums! Of course, we were all flashing our cameras in order to capture such a sight.

Unfortunately, I was over-enthusiastic and managed to loose one of my sandals down the embankment. When I say bare bums, it was much more. Each and every bottom was ornately tattooed with various designs, which obviously carried a message. It caused a few giggles at my expense from the other tourists but I won't dwell too long on such minor mishaps. As we recovered from the shock of it all we were led back to the village to enjoy a concert.

This concert was really fabulous. I have been to several but this was far superior to any I had seen before. The Chief came forward for *whaik rero*, (an oration), a talk about their traditions and to try to teach us some of their language. We saw some of the significant customs, such as the traditional Maori *hongi* (greeting) – hands are clasped and the noses lightly touched together.

The young women performed various dances and the warriors performed the *haka* – the dance that is usually performed before NZ rugby matches. They chant, stride forward sideways, flash their eyes while sticking out their tongues. I should mention here that all the girls and warriors were very ornately tattooed. The entertainment lasted for around an hour, a remarkable show of their culture. Later, we were lead into a big tent and served our dinner, the one cooked in the ground! It was absolutely delicious, so we all heaved a sigh of relief.

When dinner was over and we thought that the evening had come to an end, we were given a torch each and were lead outside in the forest again. I must say, the balmy evening air and the wonderful smell of the ferns was a real delight. When we reached a certain point we were all instructed to turn off our torches and – low and behold – we saw glow worms all around us like beautiful silver stars in the sky. It truly was a really magical experience. The walk was rounded off by being taken to a lake where there was an amazing display of volcanic explosions. We all agreed that the whole evening had been excellent!

Our next stop was Lake Taupo, a really large lake of outstanding beauty where we stayed in a lovely hotel overlooking the water. As ever, the place had many attractions to enjoy and when staying for only just one night, there is never enough time to sample everything, but at least my friends had a fleeting chance to get a feel of this wonderful country.

Then on to Napier, the town we had visited for the Art Deco Festival last year. I was delighted to see how impressed Jackie and Ted were to see the wonderful architecture of this town. A real delight.

Our final destination on the North Island was Paraparaumu Beach, where Sue and family live. Naturally, Sue was delighted to see old friends and to 'show off' her area. She took us for a walk along the beach, which stretches for miles and like all NZ beaches, was practically deserted! A very rare experience in England.

The next day, we boarded the ferry to cross to the South Island.

Normally, this would have been a delightful experience but the weather wasn't kind to us, so we stayed in the cabin for three hours.

Our first stop on the South Island was Kaikoura, famous for its whales and dolphins. Offshore, the sea bed drops away rapidly to the Kaikoura Canyon, 1,000 metres deep and a kilometre from land, attracting a large variety of sea mammals. Whale watching and swimming with dolphins have become big business here, and the presence of expectant tourists has spawned a number of eco-oriented businesses offering swimming with seals, sea kayaking, scuba diving, hiking and even sky watching. My friends chose to go for the whale watching.

Nearly home and our next stop was Hanmer Springs. The drive from Kaikoura to Hanmer is absolutely fabulous, leading up and around mountains, unfolding into lush meadows; a really spectacular sight.

After touring Australia in a Camper van before coming to NZ, my friends were overjoyed to relax in the therapeutic delight of the thermal pools. Can you imagine the joy of sitting in a comforting, outdoor hot pool while looking at the majestic mountains and blue sky?

The final journey was home here to Christchurch where, during the next few weeks, I duly showed them the customary itinerary of sites plus something on their last evening that even I hadn't tried before.

Christchurch has an amazing old tram system running through the town. It's really good for the tourists because apart from riding on this vehicle from the 1930s, the driver gives an informative commentary as it travels along. You can alight at any stop and rejoin it when you are ready to visit somewhere else. In the evening, a special restaurant tram is used. Dinner is served while the tram rides around and diners are able to witness the nightlife of Christchurch. That, in itself, is a joke, since there hardly seems to be any nightlife and we saw very few people walking around. I suppose they were all in bed. It really was quite amusing as the tram track is limited and we were riding around and around the same circuit over and over again. However, it was a lovely dinner and something different to end a holiday.

I am now on the eve of my visit back to England. I must say that emigrating has been a rollercoaster experience. This last year has seen me taking over a property that was bought for me by my daughter – without my actually seeing it, yet I absolutely love it in spite of all the work it needed to restore it to its former glory. And now, at last, after much stress, I've finished the job and am feeling very relieved and happy about it all.

Much to my delight, I have had a wonderful flow of visitors from England who actually made the long haul journey to visit me. This has been more than I could have expected or hoped for, and for which I have felt very privileged.

All this in my first year here, which makes me feel so very grateful for all the help, loving support and advice I have had from everyone, including my own two girls and their families. Also, I must make a special mention of all the gentlemen visitors, who have been mending, fixing and generally looking for odd jobs that I might have needed help with – all of which has made my new home more comfortable and cosy.

'Happiness is as a butterfly which, when pursued, is always just beyond our grasp, but which, if you will sit down quietly, may alight upon you.' (Nathaniel Hawthorne.)

I haven't had much time to 'sit quietly' since landing in NZ and I haven't consciously been pursuing happiness. I've just been going about every day, trying to make some sense of life without Colin, but, I am delighted to say, I think that that butterfly must have managed to alight upon me at some time because, quite simply, I think I am beginning to feel happy!

13

I have just returned home from a wonderful trip back home to England. I decided to visit my homeland because I wanted to visit my old friends again and feel loved, and I am delighted to say that certainly happened. Everyone, without exception, was extremely kind and I had many adventures – it's been like a shot in the arm (not that I've ever had one!).

I must confess that as the plane started to descend in England, I felt overwhelmed; it is so much prettier than I'd ever realised and I had to control my emotions about my strong sense of home-coming – of belonging.

My first stop was with my friends Sheila and Peter, who live on Shoreham Beach. I spent four wonderful days with them. They took me to Brighton and I thoroughly enjoyed the delights of an English seaside resort that had all the elegant grandeur of the Edwardian era. The wonderful squares and crescents; some still very grand while others being rendered rather squalid with the passage of time and now being a conglomeration of apartments, flats and bedsits. Regardless of that, I could still instantly imagine glorious scenes of grand ladies parading with their husbands. She in her sumptuous gown and a large hat heavily strewn with flowers, clasping a dainty lace parasol and he sporting a saucy handlebar moustache, a striped rowing blazer and straw boater. Perhaps followed subserviently by a nanny pushing the perambulator. All this accompanied by the intoxicating strains of a brass band playing Gilbert and Sullivan!

A trip around the Sussex villages made me realise what I had missed so much apart from my friends; the leafy English lanes, village greens, duck ponds, the ancient churches and their bells, welcoming country pubs, Tudor houses, thatched cottages, oast houses – the list was endless. Although beautiful in so many ways, NZ simply doesn't have the quaintness of old England.

My next stop was in Kent, my home county, and to the comfort of my friends Jackie and Ted's home. I was very lucky that they allowed me to have a key and a bed and the freedom to come and go as I pleased, thus enabling me to meet up with my many friends.

I also had a wonderful opportunity to visit my most beloved area – the Cotswolds, where Colin was born and bred. We loved visiting the area so much that we were content to return again and again, each year. My friends Elizabeth and Tom took me to stay in the most imaginative place called The Watermark, which was a private village built round the Isis and Windrush lakes. From there, we ventured forth to absorb the delights of one of the prettiest areas in England. My list of what I miss most about England was growing rapidly. Cotswold buildings built in that gentle peachy-coloured stone, surrounded by their old English country gardens complete with rambling roses, hollyhocks, lupins, foxgloves etc. And, of course, dovecotes. As we drove along, even the surrounding countryside with its gracious willows, hawthorn hedges, cow parsley, daisies, dandelions and bluebells was an absolute delight.

I was so overjoyed to see it all again that I couldn't refrain from bursting into song! I started with the Shakespeare's song 'Now is the month of Maying, When merry lads, are playing, fa a la la la la la la la! fa a la la la la la la! Each with his bonny lass, A-dancing on the grass, fa a la la la!' etc. From that straight into Schubert's 'Trout Song'; 'I stood beside a brooklet that sparkled on its way, and there beneath the wavelets a tiny trout at play. As swiftly as an arrow he darted to and fro, the gayest of the fishes among the reeds below.' Of course, on seeing some daffodils, I just had to break into Wordsworth's 'Daffodils'; 'I wandered lonely as a cloud, that floats on high o'er vale and hill when all at once I saw a crowd, a host of golden daffodils. Beside the lake, beneath the trees, fluttering and dancing in the breeze.' Then I saw a magnificent tree of lilac blossoms and, of course, I just had to give Ivor Novello an airing with his wonderful 'We'll gather lilacs in the spring again, we'll walk together down and English lane.' By the time we reached the source of the River Thames in a Trewsbury meadow, I grandly belted forth the very patriotic song, 'Old Father Thames' as my very refined friends shouted 'Oh, shut up!'

I also visited the Chelsea Flower Show, so all in all I was overjoyed with things that we English often take for granted. When I visited the crematorium, I chose to take a bunch of wild cow parsley blooms from the hedgerows instead of taking a bunch of commercially grown flowers. It seemed the right thing to do since Colin so admired the natural beauty of the countryside, especially the very delicate cow parsley.

I was pleased to visit Rochester and the Dickens Festival, this time as a tourist! I must say, I was very surprised to receive a call from the council who had heard I was back in the UK, asking me if I would like to make an appearance in one of my shows! Although I had the full support of my friends, I felt it presented too many worries, so I declined, nevertheless it was a tremendous boost to my confidence and the kudos it brought was very comforting. I was even mentioned on the radio!

I spent an interesting day walking around and marvelling at the Norman castle and cathedral, as I'd always done in the past. They are certainly the grandest buildings in the city and I hope that Rochester will always be a treasured place for visitors, even though the surrounding area is somewhat bedraggled.

I spent several weekends with my very good friends Helen and Dean and their children. Helen and Dean are part of the Oast

House Theatre group and I was able to enjoy several productions and meet old acquaintances. I simply love the atmosphere of that old converted Oast House.

By the time I hit London I had developed into a typical tourist, frantically snapping pictures of Horse Guards Parade and other such sights! London must be one of the grandest cities in the world. Everything about it is exciting, but having been snoozing away in peaceful NZ for the past fourteen months, I was really shocked at the volume of people and traffic. NZ and UK are practically the same size. The UK has a population of 66 million. NZ has a population of 4 million.

In London I did just about everything a tourist loves to do – marvel at the ancient buildings, watch the pageantry of the guards – see four shows – hit the shops! My friends jokingly told me that Marks and Spencer went into a decline when I left the UK, but I think I've put things right for them again now! I also had a very interesting ride on the Docklands Light Railway, but some of it was closed because an unexploded WW2 bomb had been found – fancy that! I resolved to spend a whole day whizzing around on it the next time I visited.

One of the last expeditions I made was to France with my friends Marion and Bob. I enjoyed a visit to La Touquet, but surprisingly more to Ypres with its many memories of WW1. In four great battles around the city, over 250,000 soldiers were killed. More than 100,000 men have no known graves, of whom 54,896 are commemorated by name on the Menin Gate. If, like me, you can't quite comprehend the vastness of these numbers, it is a most amazing experience to see the rows and rows of gravestones. I actually counted 119 cemeteries on the map, all in the same area. It really puts you into an emotional turmoil, and I find it very hard to put into words the great sorrow I felt creeping over me. Although incredibly sad, there was something wonderful about the place.

On returning to the UK, I experienced the joy of seeing the White Cliffs of Dover and realised just how much relief and comfort the men who returned from the war must have felt seeing them again.

I felt very proud to think that my own husband had been in the RAF and flown Lancaster Bombers during the war and had been brave enough to do 'his bit' in spite of the fact that, as a medical student, he was exempt.

Every day was filled with the much sought-after company of my friends and each and every one of them made my visit an absolute joy. I felt such overwhelming gratitude to everyone.

I've gone through a lot of changes, states of mind, and have reached a different understanding of myself. I can't deny my heritage, I don't want to, I'm British. More than that – I'm English, and all the beauty of the world will never diminish that for me, my life has changed and I now have a new country to adjust to. NZ is incredibly beautiful in a different way and there is so much to see and enjoy here too. I have found my constant pondering about what I should do in various situations quite exhausting. I've been swaying like a boat in the wake of a larger vessel, but now I feel as though I'm settling. I'm calm at last, and I'm going to focus on my new life. I really can't postpone it any longer; I've finally reached a state of acceptance.

The journey home to my adopted country was worsened by the fact that I felt like a bag lady. While everyone else who travels business class seems to do it in style and have no need to pick up bargains, I was struggling on, bumping and knocking people with my load of goodies.

The only thing that rather worried me was when I collected one of my cases at the other end, one of the locks had been broken. I was worried about going through customs because I have heard stories of how people hide drugs etc. in the cases of other unsuspecting travellers. I struggled through customs with no problem whatsoever but I continued to worry that some unscrupulous person would come round to my house to retrieve the stash they had cleverly hidden! I had another surprise. Since I travel business class, as you might expect I often sit next to businessmen and, on this occasion, I was seriously chatted up by two of them, one on the way out and one on the way back. What a liberty! They weren't blind and deaf either and I certainly didn't give them my details, although both gave me theirs – and that's all that they're going to give me!

14

Returning home from a glorious English summer, I find that winter is well and truly here in NZ. The locals say it is the hardest winter for many years, but I find it quite pleasant outside because although it's cold, it's fresh and crisp and the sun continues to shine. Inside is another matter and I am really missing the centrally heated houses of England. At sixty-five years old, this is the first time I have ever worn fleecy-lined vests and long johns! I have even resorted to wearing woollen gloves indoors, so that indicates how very cold it is. I look like some sort of Victorian granny, huddled up in all those clothes.

The scenery, as ever, is amazing. The Southern Alps, which are the backbone of the South Island, are covered in snow. I sometimes walk along the beach and thank God for all the beauty around me. Imagine looking at the sea ablaze with the morning sun and the majestic snow-capped mountains rising into the bright blue sky beyond. It really is awe-inspiring.

The interesting thing is that, in spite of the extreme cold, the flowers persist in blooming. I have passed many gardens where trees are heavy with blossom and geraniums are still climbing over walls and fences. I have a pink camellia in full bloom; a wonderful sight in the depths of dreary winter. Jan and Andrew took me for a ride up into the mountains to view the ski fields. I had no idea that the area would be so busy. In addition to skiing, folk were tobogganing down hills and skating on frozen lakes. The locals really seem to enjoy themselves when the snow comes. We passed a place called Castle Hill, which has a really interesting rock formation and was featured in the film of *Lord of the Rings*. I also saw the mountain parrot, the kea, a beautiful bird with green and blue feathers and a flash of bright red under the wings. Unfortunately, it is very bold and really destructive. It fearlessly investigates the visiting trucks and cars and when I tried to take a good picture of it in action on some unfortunate person's car bonnet, it started to squawk at me and waddle towards my camera in a rather threatening manner.

The adult sheep here are now making the most awful baa-ing noise which sounds just like some huge uncouth burp. It was explained to me that they are calling for their lost lambs – that is, lost to the butcher. Apparently they are usually killed between three to six months, so the chops you buy and eat really are very young lambs. Chops named 'hogget' are from lambs twelve months old. All horribly upsetting, isn't it? Fortunately, I have never liked the taste of lamb so at least I can sleep at night!

It reminds me of the time when I was entertaining with my after-dinner talks and on one occasion was booked to entertain a group of businessmen and their wives. I always tried to focus my talk on things appertaining to the audience so on this occasion, with the butcher in mind, I told them this story, 'I have been asked to sing on many different occasions, one being the local butcher's funeral. I was also given free choice with the music, so I thought it rather appropriate on this occasion to sing "Now ye sheep can safely graze".' Fortunately, they could see the fun in this.

I have joined another club. This one is the Federation of Graduate Women. Hopefully I can look forward to some rousing discussion group meetings. But, and this is the most amazing thing ever, I have also joined something that I would never have thought possible ... a gym! I can hardly believe it myself. All my life I have hated physical exercise, always preferring a good book and a glass of

A LEAP INTO THE UNKNOWN

wine, but suddenly I have developed the quite unexpected urge to get myself fit and well. Let me tell you about the place. It has nine chairs set in a circle and between each chair is a pad on the floor. The idea is that you sit on a chair and do whatever exercise is required of you and then, when an announcement says 'change stations', you jump onto the pad in between the chairs and start running on the spot before you change stations again onto the next chair.

All this to the most loud, stimulating, pulsating music, which I have always disliked but I now find strangely inspiring. While on each chair, you are either wrestling with weights or heaving yourself into all sorts of contortions, flinging your legs all over the place. Everything I have always hated and yet I now love it. Great isn't it? I've actually started sweating too. I stagger out of the place feeling somewhat shell shocked but invigorated and ready for anything.

I read this advertisement in the local paper recently. It has to be the best singles ad ever printed:

> SINGLE BLACK FEMALE seeks male companionship, ethnicity unimportant. I'm a very good looking girl who loves to play, loves long walks in the woods, riding in your pick-up truck, hunting, camping and fishing trips, cosy nights lying by the fire. Candlelight dinners will have me eating out of your hand. I'll be at the front door when you get home from work, wearing only what nature gave me. Call 404 875 6420 and ask for Daisy, I'll be waiting ...

Over 15,000 men found themselves talking to the Atlanta Humane Society about an eight-week old black Labrador retriever.

I've been going up to bed very early in the evening, but if you could see the house and feel the cold without central heating, I am sure you would do the same! I can't see much difference between watching TV or reading downstairs in the sitting room or upstairs in a lovely cosy bed!

Friends have been kind enough to show concern about my solitary life and I thank them for that. It isn't so alarming for me, since I am an 'only' child and right from early years I have had to accept being alone and amusing myself. I am an avid reader and have been occupied quite contentedly, so it really hasn't been such a difficult change to accept.

Here is the good news. It appears that, at last, I am beginning to get out and about in the local society. I can now list several clubs that I attend:
1. The Over-Seas League (full of ex-pats like myself);
2. The Christchurch Club (a rather dated club trying to keep its end up but nevertheless it has the occasional interesting function);
3. The Federation of University Graduate Women (interesting speakers and discussion groups);
4. The University of the Third Age (U3A) – very similar to the above, but with men too;
5. A music appreciation group (where all the dear old ladies sit, drink tea, eat cakes and talk loudly over the music being played. Not quite what I considered it would be, but hoping to eventually get the general chit-chat around to music!);
6. Bridge;
7. The Gym! Yes! Amazing;
8. Yoga;
9. And my latest – Mahjong.

A kind lady asked me if I would like to learn to play Mahjong. She invited me to her house along with two other friends and they spent an afternoon teaching me how to play the game. Later in the week, we all met at the Christchurch Club where they run a weekly meeting for ladies to play. And, guess what? I won every game. Of course, it was only luck, because I really don't know how I did it, but it was good for my kudos. I rather enjoy the game and look forward to having a regular weekly event to attend.

I also get the occasional unexpected invitation to lunch or go to a show or concert with other people I have met along the way. So, things are looking up for me and I am getting out and about. I also have the garden!

I remind myself of one of those circus performers who spin plates – and just as soon as he has every one of them up and spinning, he has to run to the first to keep it all going. I continue to discover that there is such a lot going on in Christchurch.

Of course, it is very comforting to know that Jan is just round the corner. She rings occasionally or calls to take me out to lunch or dinner, as well as the horse events, which I am now beginning to thoroughly enjoy. I'm even equipped with a shooting stick that originally belonged to Colin, so I have part of him with me too. I now accept how odd I was looking trotting around in my usual 'city' clothes complete with high heels and handbag. One day was so cold that I actually had to borrow some fleecy lined-leggings that Jan straps around the horses legs. That caused quite a stir!

The horse events are shaping up very nicely. They start at 6.15 a.m. when Jan picks me up in the truck. We then drive to the paddock to load the horse. I'm sure he is obstinate because he always seems to be right at the very top of the field, which means that poor old Jan has quite a trudge up the mountain to get him. The events are always held some way out of town. Jan has now given me a list of jobs to do on arrival at the venue, the first being to sweep out the truck, the inside of which is filled with the overwhelming smell of horse droppings plus sweat and bad breath. Next job is to prepare the horse by brushing his tail and painting his hooves. I then generally hand Jan bits and pieces as she needs them and even polish her boots as she sits in the saddle! How's that for love and devotion? Once all the jobs are done, everybody usually walks the cross country course in order to familiarise themselves with what is required. The dressage and show jumping are always set out the same way so need no further investigation. I thoroughly enjoy walking the course, but my idea of enjoying it is to saunter, so invariably the competitors pass me still going out as they are on their way back!

The jumps fill me with horror. Apart from the various heights, some have little dykes beside them, which require the horse to jump even higher and stretch more. One jump had a tall hedge with a sort of keyhole opening in it, which the horse had to negotiate before actually going straight into the jump. I worry that Jan might come off but she tells me she really enjoys it, although I can't see her smiling much when she's doing it. She looks like she's filled with terror!

The events are quite sociable with people gathering in each other's trucks to discuss the day's activities. When I first went, I used to serve smoked salmon and salad plus other goodies just for the two of us, but now friendships have been formed, I am pleased to invite others to join our picnic. I absolutely love doing it all and enjoy the camaraderie and jolly atmosphere. A bit like the open-air concerts we used to do in the UK, only in the back of a smelly old truck!

The last event was particularly pleasurable. The course started in a pine forest and it was an absolute delight to walk on a bed of pine needles amongst trees so old that their roots were spreading out like old gnarled fingers on the surface. The perfume was overwhelming and there were tons of beautiful pine cones scattered around the place. Apparently, the locals gather them for their log burners, but the thought of burning them seems such a terrible waste to me. I could see garden centres spraying them gold or silver at Christmas and making a great profit. The whole scenario was outstandingly beautiful with the low sun touching the early morning dew and transforming it into little diamonds. Yes, I must confess that much to my own amazement, I am really getting into the country ways now.

Jan had asked me if I would allow her to entertain, in my house, her many friends for a mid-winter celebration (the equivalent of a Christmas dinner in the UK). She assured me that no-one can decorate a house as well as me, and, of course, flattery gets one everywhere! As ever, I drew the line at cooking. All was fine since each couple elected to bring a different course of the meal, which seemed to go on forever so in the final analysis, no-one had complete responsibility for the evening. As ever, I 'went to town' and had a snow and ice theme with my usual silver decorations and white lights over the big mirror in the sitting room and a white table also festooned with snow and ice decorations. Even I thought I had excelled myself. I actually dressed up as an old-fashioned waitress, all in black with a white apron and hat and served the food. That caused a laugh, but I felt I owed it to Jan, since when she and Sue were teenagers and we used to have dinner parties, they used to do the same for me, the only difference being that they wore short skirts with black stockings and suspenders! It always caused a stir and, much to their delight, the gentlemen guests often tipped them. Unfortunately that didn't happen in my case. I wonder if it was something to do with my age and, dare I say, my face and figure?

Nevertheless, it was an extremely successful evening and everyone seemed to thoroughly enjoy themselves.

'There must have been times more exciting than this, but I can't quite recall them.' (Unknown.)

The emotional fog is beginning to clear and I am feeling much brighter, although I still hanker after Colin, my friends and the life we had in Kent, which I still miss so much. Just because there is so much that is truly wonderful here, it doesn't mean that I wouldn't rather have things as they were. It's incredibly hard 'letting go'.

15

Quite suddenly, spring is here! The weather is warm and balmy and everywhere is festooned with blossoms. Only last week, it was cold and blustery and I could actually hear the thunderous sea pounding into the shore from my bedroom. Now, all is quiet and calm and fleecy lined vests are a thing of the past.

I saw the most beautiful sight while driving into town. I drove past the Pacific Ocean, sparkling silver in the low sun, people out and about walking along the golden sands. I continued the drive to where the River Avon starts to meander through the very heart of the city. All the weeping willows were graciously trailing their lush leaves into the water and as I looked along the river, I saw two black swans with a family of five signets gliding along. It was a truly lovely sight to see. The contrast of the fresh green leaves of the willows and the shiny black of the bird's feathers was so vibrant, all enhanced by the fact that I was playing a Chopin CD at the time. Utter bliss! And for a moment, I felt quite overcome with the beauty of it all.

Unfortunately, on returning home, something was waiting in my letterbox which broke the spell. It was a civil defence pamphlet informing me what I should collect as an emergency survival kit in the event of an earthquake, eruption, tsunami etc. I suppose this didn't surprise me too much since only a few weeks earlier, due to the torrential rain, there had been a landslide just at the end of my road.

I am getting on well with the Mahjong. Although I have only been three times, I have won the kitty each time! This is not by skill; I just don't know how I've done it. There are Mahjong manuals and it is acceptable to have them on your lap and refer to them during play. At present, I have no manual to refer to and therefore I have been going with the flow, and actually winning. I don't know the answer, but I now feel almost afraid to buy and refer to a manual. Will it break my spell of good luck?

During the last month I have been to two performances at our local professional theatre and both have truly been excellent. The first was a Shakespearean evening full of verse, madrigals and singing of the sonnets. It was such a delight that I thought, for a minute, I was back in our beloved Stratford upon Avon. The second was a play set in a local village hall in a backwater of New Zealand in the early 1960s, and brought back many memories of the trials and tribulations of early love at the local village social events. It was so very funny, but at the same time rather poignant. Why does life always seem to be a struggle? Anyway, I wended my way home thinking how comfortable I felt with the age I've reached now, so that can't be bad.

'Success can only be measured in terms of distance travelled.' (Mavis Grant.)

Now for some outrageous news – well, it is to me! As you know, due to my illness, I have no hair anywhere. I now have had some eyebrows tattooed on! It was suggested to me by a friend, who assured me it would look natural. I was rather hesitant at first, but eventually plucked up the courage to do so. I must say, I like my new eyebrows and feel very pleased with them. The fact is, I never could pencil them in properly. One day I would look as though I was feeling very bad tempered and another I would look as though I had stuck my finger in an electric socket, so with all that inconsistency I am so glad to be looking normal again. It's early days yet. I have been told to expect some itching and flaking, but as long as my forehead doesn't drop down over my eyes, I think I can cope!

I popped up to the North Island this month to visit Sue and the family. The boys seem to be growing so quickly and it is at times like this that I realise my main reason for being here.

I recently flew down to Queenstown for the Blossom Festival and spent a pleasant week with my friends Alfred and Barbara. It was a lovely trip, but now I am becoming familiar with all the surrounding areas of the South Island, even that doesn't hold the thrill it used to. Fortunately for them, they came here by choice and instantly loved it all, but one must remember they also have each other. Unfortunately I can't seem to feel the same enthusiasm as them. I can appreciate all that I have and the incredible beauty of it all, but my heart is still in Kent and the life I had there. I wonder if I'll ever feel any different.

At present Jan and Andrew are away for a month visiting the UK and Italy. Although we certainly aren't in each other's pockets, I must say that I miss them. Just to know they are round the corner is a great comfort to me, also a safety net. I call into their house everyday and spend a couple of hours reading a book with their cat on my lap. I feel so sorry for the poor thing being alone in the house for so long and obviously wondering where they are. With soothing purrs drifting up from the little ball of fluff curled cosily on my lap, we are mutually comforting each other.

On a lighter note, I have just returned from having a 'top up' tattooing of my eyebrows. It's all part of an on-going treatment. The therapist says that she doesn't like to make them too dark from the beginning but to do it in stages, so that you know when they are a shade that suits you. Since mine make me look like Groucho Marks right now, I feel that I won't need to go back again. Admittedly they do seem to fade a little after a week or so, but for the time being I think I can safely say enough is enough!

The last month has been amazing for me. It seems as though I have been 'discovered' and am now in the real world again.

I went along to a ladies' luncheon at the Christchurch Club and noticed someone I didn't recognise come into the room for the pre-lunch drinks. Knowing just how difficult it can be, being alone, I immediately approached her and started talking. We got on so well that we continued our conversation and sat next to each other at the lunch. It's quite usual for most NZ people to ask immigrants why they are here and what they think of the country, so when asked, I gave her my run-down on what I thought of NZ and the government etc. Half way through the lunch we decided to exchange cards and I was horrified to find that she was an Honourable Lady and a Member of Parliament! It didn't finish there. A few days later I was at a ladies' dinner and again spotted a dear little old lady and decided to do my Christian act of being friendly. She asked my name and where I was living, so I said; 'My name is Sumner and I live in Sumner, so you may call me Lady Sumner.' She laughed and remarked that when Sumner was named all those years ago, it was obviously in preparation for my coming. It was just then that someone passed by and said, 'Good evening, Lady Isaac.' Cringe! Cringe! Another clanger dropped!

Actually, she was very gracious about it and said that she already knew of me due to my earlier meeting with the other Lady a few days before. I wonder what was said. To complete the story, a few days later the telephone rang and a voice asked if I would accept a call from Lady Isaac. Now if I had been in England, I would have made some silly remark thinking it was one of my friends having a joke. Thankfully, I didn't say anything awful but just 'Yes, of course'. Lady Isaac came on the phone and said she had been thinking about me and would I mind if she passed my telephone number onto a friend of hers who also lives in Sumner. So you see – I am now moving in exulted circles!

Someone else I met at another dinner was the wife of the local undertaker. We also got on well together and she told me how her firm are sponsors for various events in and around Christchurch and that they were due at a prize giving function in Sumner the next Sunday, suggesting I might like to accompany them as their guest. Naturally, I was pleased to join them, but was rather shocked to know that it was at Andrew's bowls club, so when I went along, instead of being with the hoi polloi as usual, I was with the crème de la crème sponsors. Jan thought that highly amusing and asked me if I could do a deal with them for when I depart this earth! Summer has arrived in NZ now and, in spite of avoiding the sun, I have already caught it! It's still so very strange for me to know that Christmas is just round the corner, especially when the TV adverts are a mixture of Christmas goodies and sun tan protection creams or lotions. They have Santa Parades in all the towns around NZ, which seems so odd in the sunshine.

'Once again we come to the holiday season, a deeply religious time that each of us observes, in his own way, by going to the mall of his choice.' (Dave Barry.)

Although I thought I had finished getting the house the way I wanted, I've just had a conservatory built alongside the sitting room and I am very pleased with it. I must tell you about the gentlemen who built it for me. They were real characters – a bit like Del Boy and Rodney from *Only Fools and Horses*. They gave me one of their business cards – here goes:

> Professional Killers – World Travellers – Double Agents
> One Night Stand Kings – Soft Shoe Dancers
> Public Relations Extra Ordinaire – River Boat Gamblers
> Soldiers of Fortune and Last of the Big Time Spenders
> Zane and Shane
> Space Journeys – Bridges Destroyed – Wars Fought
> Tigers Tamed – Revolutions Started – Bars Emptied
> Governments Run – Orgies Organised – Uprisings Quelled
> Football Games Fixed – Dinosaurs Neutered
> And always available for a beer.

By the time they finished the job I was really sorry to see them go because they had been incredibly witty and such fun. I hadn't laughed so much in ages. They asked me what I thought of the card as they were just about to have another batch printed. I told them that I thought something very important was missing and that it should include 'toy boys' – not that I required that service, I was quick to add.

In NZ, when all the work is completed it is customary to have something called a 'roof shout'. This is an occasion when all who had anything to do with the building are invited along for drinks and nibbles. Another chap involved was called Wayne, and his wife Jayne is a friend of Jan's, so they were included too. I remarked to Jan how confusing it could be because we will have Zane, Shane, Wayne and Jayne!

The Christchurch Club recently had a military dinner and I was invited to attend wearing Colin's RAF medals. I wasn't quite sure about it, but they assured me that they thought Colin would be proud of me representing him. It was grand occasion with all the ex-servicemen in their special military evening suits complete with medals. I carried a picture of Colin taken at Buckingham Palace in my handbag, so that I could show anyone who asked about him. It was a rather special occasion for me, since I felt it was keeping his memory alive.

At one of the ladies' lunches, we were talking about music and I mentioned Colin's vast collection of over 500 CDs and my own equally extensive collection of DVDs and videos including most of the grand operas, Gilbert and Sullivan operettas, many of the famous singers in concert, Shakespeare plays and other great works of art and literature. The group I was sitting with were so impressed that they asked if they could call around and see some of them. As a result of this, we have formed a group that we are calling The Sumner Soirees because it is held in my house, which is in Sumner. By popular request, we meet every month. Ever the teacher, it is giving me so much pleasure planning the programmes for each meeting, rotating through music, art, literature, biography, history etc. Everyone brings buffet food and some nibbles and I open the wine, which I am expert at. We all sit around having a lovely time. I am so happy about it because since arriving in NZ and not knowing anyone, I have been watching these DVDs by myself, which, of course, it is not as pleasurable as sharing the experience and now I have like-minded ladies to enjoy it all with.

'To be happy at home is the ultimate result of all ambition.' (Oscar Levant.)

16

Christmas has come and gone this year and I am left wondering if I will ever truly be able to rescue and enjoy the festive spirit again. When Colin was so ill at Christmas time, I announced that I was cancelling Christmas from now on. Thankfully, I am beginning to feel a little better and I just can't ignore such an important festival. I ended up decorating three Christmas trees! I decorated one for Jan and another two for Sue when I went the North Island to spend the holiday with her family.

'Twas the night before Christmas, when all through the house
Not a creature was stirring, not even a mouse,
The stockings were hung by the chimney with care,
In the hopes that St Nicholas soon would be there.'
From 'A Visit from St Nicholas' (Clement Clarke Moore.)

And something more up to date; 'We expect too much at Christmas. It's got to be magical. It's got to go right. Feasting, fun. The perfect present. All that anticipation. Take it easy. Love's the thing. The rest is tinsel.' (Pam Brown.)

Talk of Christmas reminds of the times gone by when we used to play silly parlour games. It was such fun, but one I liked in particular was picking just one word that you considered would describe you, and then the rest of the company revealing which word they thought best described you. My grandson said the word for me was 'eccentric'! What a cheek. I prefer 'bohemian' which according to the dictionary means 'A person, artistic or intellectual, who lives and acts unconventionally.' It certainly started a debate when people couldn't agree with what others thought of them.

I still find it really odd to be celebrating Christmas in the middle of the summer, but the weather was wet and windy so it almost felt like being in England again. We have had a dreadful summer with icy gale force winds and torrential rain. The locals say they have never known such strange weather conditions. I hear UK conditions are similar and realise that the unusual weather conditions seem to be global, I find the whole thing rather alarming.

Flying up to Sue's has become quite a regular occurrence and it makes me realise just how much my life has changed. Being English, one always associates travel with cars, buses and trains but here, air travel and airports have replaced railway stations for me.

Quite suddenly, I am feeling so much more at home here. It is two years this week since I left England, so I suppose it's about time too! Making new friends has made a tremendous difference and organising the Sumner Soirees for my group of ladies has brought me a great deal of pleasure.

It gives me the chance to bring a little joy and inspiration to others, reminiscent of my entertaining and teaching days, only with people who actually want to listen and learn! I spontaneously sang a little ditty at a dinner party a few months back and I seem to have received several further invitations on the strength of it! They seem to enjoy the novelty and have even started requesting their favourites, which seem to be 'Have Some Madeira M'dear' and 'Only a Glass of Champagne' so I suppose they know what they like. I have shown them the video of my last performance in England, which they seemed to find amusing!

I have started to learn to sing a few Maori folk songs. I continue to go to the U3A meetings and at the last one we had the Head of the Christchurch Waterboard giving a talk. On the whole, it was pretty boring but one point I found incredible was that the two places in the world with the purest mountain water are Evian, which

A LEAP INTO THE UNKNOWN

as you know is bottled, and Christchurch, so it's good to know that we get that for free.

Just recently one of Jan's friends, who breeds and trains horses, rang to tell us that one of her mares was about the give birth and we dashed in the car to see the event. It was so exciting to actually witness the birth. It was fascinating to watch the dear little creature try to stand up on such long, wobbly legs. When we returned a few weeks later, it was so delightful to see it jumping and skipping around the field.

Just before Christmas, I was invited to go to the Christchurch Races, and I must confess that my first thoughts were of Ascot, but I was very pleasantly surprised. It was every bit as stylish as Ascot and ran to form in all other ways too – magnificent horses, exciting races, ladies in beautiful outfits and outrageous hats, flowing champagne and picnic hampers etc. The people who invited me had access to the club and members' stand and later, another gentleman invited me into the committee room, so that rather heightened the grandeur of the occasion. It was almost comparable to the Royal Enclosure!

Last year I was lucky enough to have three groups of visitors from the UK and I am looking forward to four this year! Add to that the occasional visit from Sue's family and the grandsons Chris, Wes and Oliver on separate occasions, plus Alfred and Barbara from further south and I rarely seem to be by myself for too long.

Apart from the spectacular scenery, the Pacific Ocean, the vineyards etc. I consider Christchurch's major attractions are the Gondola and the old trams. I have been 'up the Gondola' and 'round the trams' ten times with visitors already! I purchased a season ticket last year and have renewed it this year in preparation for the forthcoming visitors. You might think I would get tired of it, but I actually really love it! The locals think it's hilarious – some have never even been on the Gondola, an example of how people tend not to appreciate their habitat. Another thing that I have done many times is drive to the top of the mountain and then round the summit. I must confess that it was rather hair-raising the first couple of times, but I have really developed great confidence. I think the locals are surprised that a sweet little old granny like me is 'up for it all', as the young folk say.

As December and January are the main 'summer' holidays it seems impossible to get any tradesmen in because they are all off to some beach! This hasn't worked out too well for me these last weeks because I developed an outrageous toothache and had dreadful trouble in seeing a dentist. Due to the holiday, everyone was fully booked and I had to go on an emergency list. I had an abscess in the gum which lead to the tooth being removed. Worse still, at the follow-up appointment I was told that I would need a further two teeth out! How awful to lose so many in such a short space of time, and that was not all I lost. The dental fees here are colossal. At $217 a tooth, I nearly needed to mortgage the house! It appears to be more expensive to live in New Zealand, health-wise. I also pay several hundred dollars a year to see a dermatologist for my 'mole map'.

In addition to all that, it costs approximately $50 for a general doctor's appointment. Not good news as you age and bits start to fester and fall off!

'You know you're getting older when you try to straighten out the wrinkles in your socks and discover that you're not wearing any.' (Leonard L. Knott.)

'They tell you that you'll lose your mind when you grow older. What they don't tell you is that you won't miss it very much.' (Malcolm Cowley.)

Getting back to the teeth, I already had an idea that things were going wrong and at sixty-five, I suppose I just have to accept it. I now have no teeth in my bottom jaw, so will have to have new dentures which are estimated at $2,500. I have been without teeth for a couple of weeks while all the swelling settles down. I have a temporary denture to put in, but it is far too painful just now. The only consolation is that I am now losing weight again, only this time because I simply can't eat anything other than porridge, soft fruit and cottage cheese. Oh well – that's life! My mouth may have caved in and my chin is rising up to touch the tip of my nose, but my body still looks good!

I've recently unpacked my Victorian birdcage, which I intend to hang in the new conservatory. I needed a couple of artificial feather birds to hang in it, and had noticed that there was a 'Christmas' shop permanently open in Christchurch and thought what business could they possibly do all year round? But that might be the very place to find the birds, so I ventured forth to see what they had, and what a surprise I got! It was absolutely fantastic. A grotto containing a vast selection of Christmas trees decorated in so many different styles plus all the paraphernalia one associates with the festive season. The owners were great collectors and had many antique decorations which they had incorporated in the most wonderful display. They told me that they even open to visitors by appointment in the evenings, when the lights are prettier and invited me to view it all. What a delight!

They had made a route to follow and, in moving along, each area was triggered into action, sweet music was played and there was so much to look at. It really was a wonderful fairyland. I asked why they were permanently open and realised that another little detail about NZ life had escaped me. The festive season is celebrated twice in NZ! Once in December and again in June when they have the mid-winter Festival of Lights, the same as the English Christmas but without the gifts.

I was told that, apart from running the shop and the party bookings to view it all, they supplied hotels and other public places all over NZ with dressed trees and decorations, so they were always busy.

In January, one of the theatres in central Christchurch staged a production of *Guys and Dolls*. It was an amazing production, as good as any I have seen in London. Everything – set design, costumes, movement, singing and dancing – was first class. It was absolutely wonderful.

I must confess that when I moved here, I really didn't expect too much in the way of entertainment, but I have been astounded.

It was a particularly pleasant evening for me because I went with the Christchurch Club and after the show we all went back to the club for dinner, so that seemed to round the evening off very nicely.

After the most dismal summer, we are experiencing a glorious autumn – and what a relief that is, since I continue to have a steady flow of visitors from England. My friend Barbara left and three days later dear Jenny arrived, having just separated from her partner and feeling very fragile. Naturally we spent many hours discussing men, marriage and such.

'Keep your eyes wide open before marriage; half shut afterwards.' (F. Nietzsche.)

'Marriage is a mutual admiration society where one person is always in the right and the other one is the husband.' (W. Grant.)

One of my Soiree ladies, who lives in central Christchurch but has more land further north, was kind enough to invite us to visit her there. It was a large property, with a natural 'bowl' which she is in the process of turning into an amphitheatre. It was really exciting to hear her plans, see the site and imagine it filled with folk enjoying open-air concerts. It was originally a farm, but she had the farmhouse cleared away in readiness for the work to be done.

I think Jenny was quite taken back when she asked if she could use the loo and Rachel casually replied 'Yes, just behind that bush.' As Jenny walked towards it, she yelled out 'Not that one, the one next to it.' I trust she will have better facilities by the time she is up and running!

During that time, one of the Princess Line cruisers came into the port of Lyttelton, just over the mountain from Sumner. Since it is two and half times bigger than the *Titanic*, carries enough passengers and crew to fill 11 jumbo jets, has 1337 cabins, 10 restaurants, a wedding chapel, a mini-golf course, 13 bars and lounges, 2 nightclubs, shopping malls, a casino and luxury spa etc. you might get an idea of what an imposing sight it was.

We went to a concert by the NZ Symphony Orchestra in our wonderful town hall. One of my new friends, who holds a rather important position with the orchestra, invited me come along free of charge! I felt very privileged. I must say, it was a rather exhausting three weeks, but I managed to get through it. I have now been up the Gondola and round Christchurch on the trams twelve times! And I really don't mind a bit.

I now have only four days to prepare the house for my dear friends Dean and Helen and their children to visit!

17

I took Dean, Helen and their children (my fifth set of visitors this year!) to the usual local tourist attractions but as they wanted to see as much of NZ as possible, one of the first trips we made was over to the West Coast.

Since the Southern Alps run down the backbone of the South Island, it involved journeying over mountains, crossing rivers etc. and generally experiencing the feeling of being on a big dipper – with little old granny me driving!

The West Coast is an untamed costal strip of turbulent water and lush bush land, and one of the great attractions there is the area of Punakaiki and the Pancake Rocks. Here, layers of limestone have weathered to resemble an immense stack of giant pancakes producing sea caverns where the surf surges in, sending spumes of brine spouting up through vast blowholes – quite an exciting sight to see.

In the same area, we visited an old goldmine where we all panned for gold and all got a little bit, which was duly saved in a small phial for us to take home. The finding of real gold is another experience guaranteed to please the visitors, but the gentleman in charge seemed to take a fancy to me and gave me an extra portion of gold, so that brought a little giggle amongst the party. I must visit regularly – I could be a millionaire by this time next year! It was genuinely interesting to see the many goldmines in the area and how the early settlers worked and lived.

When browsing for a souvenir postcard in NZ, there is always a picture of a traffic jam, only the traffic jams here are caused by sheep and depict a lone shepherd, his dogs and hundreds of sheep running along the road. I've been held up twice before, slowly inching my way along behind them, but on this occasion it happened at just the right time because it gave my visitors chance to experience a real NZ 'traffic jam'!

After a couple of nights we came back to Christchurch, stopping at Hanmer Springs, where we all enjoyed the delights of the naturally warm pools. There is a fast-flowing river in the area and way above is a bridge, so, obviously, that is a prime area for bungee jumping – we were lucky to see one brave couple jump off the bridge while we were there. My guests thoroughly enjoyed the nearby jet boat ride, which speeds through the canyon heading for the rocks and then turning abruptly, thus causing great squeals from the passengers!

We went on to Kiakoura, where the seal colony and whale watching boats operate. Dean, Helen and family managed to capture some wonderful photographs of the whales, especially a classic shot of a whale flipping its tail and the water spraying everywhere.

We eventually travelled back to Christchurch via the vineyards, calling in for morning coffee. The vines are set in immaculate rows and I have recently been told that the posts for the rows of vines are placed by satellite, which actually directs the tractors. Modern science – astonishing, isn't it?

It was Helen's fortieth birthday while she was here, so big celebrations were planned and she was surprised to find that Sue, Jeff and the family had flown down from the North Island to join her. The day started with a champagne and salmon breakfast supplied and cooked by Jan. And then, a most unusual way to spend such a special occasion, Jan took us all to the paddock where her horse lives and we had the pleasure of a picnic, followed by jobs of Jan's choice, namely unloading bales of straw and shovelling shit! She lured us all there in order to get some help with work which needed doing! It was rather fun and since the paddock is set in an awe-inspiring position surrounded by mountains which were being grazed by sheep and cattle it was so peaceful – all this solitude with no noise other than the sounds of nature, and, of course, our excited chatter. We ended the day with a special dinner party in the evening where all twelve of us crowded around the table. I must say it was quite satisfying having so many loved ones in the house; the whole place seemed to come alive!

Since Helen's birthday was on Good Friday, we had the whole of the Easter holiday to all be together. Jan took Dean on a horsey hack, everyone else played garden games and at some point they all went paua hunting amongst the rocks of a local beach. Paua is a univalve shellfish found only in NZ coastal waters, with a unique and wonderful lustre of iridescent blues, pinks and greens. Skin divers harvest the shell with its heavy encrustation of marine growth and lime deposits, which is removed to expose the shell's full beauty. It is sold in the tourist shops, but to have gathered some naturally is a great souvenir to take home. The paua itself is like a huge black slug which is battered, fried and sold in the local fish and chip shops. I tried it once, but I think the kindest thing to say is that I didn't find it particularly palatable!

Before they left for home, we had one final trip out to Picton, at the very top of the South Island. On that occasion, we took the Coastal Pacific train. I hadn't been before and I was delighted with it – the ever-changing scenery was fascinating.

Jan and Andrew have recently bought a luxury apartment overlooking the harbour, so we were able to enjoy that too. All in all, it was very pleasant, in spite of the fact that we had to start off a 7 a.m. because the journey takes six hours but, apart from oo-ing and aa-ing at the views, we amused ourselves with my favourite card game – Phase 10 – so that kept us all happy!

As we were passing one of the many beaches on the way, there were several young boys bathing and they thought it great fun to show us their naked bottoms – they were doing 'moonies'! I quite admired their nerve!

I must say I was really feeling very weary by the time all five sets of visitors had left. I think I will have to stagger the visits in future, that way it won't be too exhausting. But it was so good to see old friends again. Now I have the house back in order and have rested, I look forward to catching up with the social life I have at last developed in Christchurch.

I was invited to a production of *Cats*. Christchurch has five theatres and so far I have only visited two of them. This production was held in the oldest and biggest theatre, built in the late 1800s and very gracious and ornate. I must confess that when I first arrived in NZ, I thought that my days of enjoying the standard of London productions were over; how wrong I was. Everything I have seen here, including the amateur productions, has been first class.

Cats was fabulous! The scenery and lighting were most imaginative and the performers were unbelievably talented. I find it astounding that such wonderful dancers can also achieve great acrobatic feats and sing beautifully too! Being English, I thought that it was a production company touring from London, but the programme (a work of art in itself) stated there were fifty-five people in the production, including the producer and technicians; twenty-eight were local Christchurch people, twenty-two were from other parts of NZ, three from other countries and two from London. The orchestra were all NZ people. Each and every one of them had qualified in some sort of university academic course, had been or was still teaching, was involved in sports and some had even represented NZ in the Olympics. One particular performer was a graduate from the National Academy of Singing and Dramatic Art with a Bachelor of Performing Arts and had experience working abroad, mainly in the UK and US. All this and yet they were all young, vibrant and good looking. It was mind-boggling! My days of making judgements concerning anything in NZ are truly over. Everything that I have been involved in, whether it be theatre, touring around, eating out or just the average day-to-day existence, I have found to be top-class. I think I am saying that I am happy with my life here.

I have had my sixty-fifth birthday recently and can hardly believe how the years are simply slipping by. The odd thing is that I still feel about forty-ish in my mind and heart – pity the body doesn't match up! I'm still having dental problems but don't seem to be losing any more weight. Crisp vegetables and apples have been impossible for me to cope with. Can the problem be that chocolate is the only thing that seems to slip down easily?

Jan keeps me involved with her horses – she has two now, so it's just more you-know-what for me to shovel up! I am really getting used to it and it is really nice to see her enjoying her hobby so much; something I would have missed if I hadn't moved here.

Lately, Jan took me to the stables while the vet gave her horse York some dental treatment. (How appropriate after what I am going through at present!) Being an ex-jockey, he was a rather small man and I thought how brave he was, since just like you or I, horses don't seem to favour dental treatment and the patient reared up several times. As the vet opened York's mouth I could see how very big his teeth were, so the equipment he used was also enormous! Extremely long files, which filled the bucket they were in. Although the brave man was pulled sideways several times, it didn't seem to bother him. I stood well back. The funny thing was, after the vet had done the job, he noticed me and enthusiastically gave me a handshake with his saliva-soaked hand! Nice!

I was involved in another adventure with three virile young men. Lucky me! My son-in-law Andrew and two others wanted to take their kayaks to a certain river and row – paddle – or whatever they call it down the river. They needed to load their kayaks onto the roof of the car, drive about two hours out of Christchurch, get into their boats and finish the race much further downstream. This is where I came in. They needed a driver to move the car from the start of their trip to the end. I was pleased to help, but I really hadn't given it much thought when I agreed. The river was absolutely miles from anywhere and I had to drive all by myself to the finishing spot. As I was driving along in the middle of nowhere, without another car or house in sight, I began to wonder what the hell I was doing! Just picture it, a sweet little old granny like me, all alone in the wilds of New Zealand. I also thought if anyone had told me on my sixtieth birthday where I would be and what I would be doing at sixty-five, I would hardly have believed it.

Once I got over my first shock and horror of being so utterly alone, I began to enjoy the tranquillity and beauty of the countryside. At the finish, I even helped them haul their kayaks up the beach. Apparently, the chaps were delighted with my help and want me to do the same again another time, so it looks as though Jan and Andrew will just have to book me well in advance since they both seem to need my favours!

Everything is jogging along fairly well, with all my visits to the theatre, symphony orchestra, opera and recitals. The Sumner Soiree continues to flourish and have even doubled in number, so I am feeling intellectually stimulated.

I continue to support Jan in her one-day horse events and am quite getting used to wellies, barbours and backpacks etc. (What are those things called 'high heels'?) In fact, it's quite enjoyable since I have a gathering of Jan's friends who come to the truck for lunch – all supplied by me but who cares, they are all lovely people.

I was even approached to become a steward by the organisers. Of course, I declined since I know nothing about the skills of riding, all I would be looking for is well-groomed horses and stylishly turned-out riders – not quite what they had in mind I think. Nevertheless, it was nice to be asked.

My friends Judy and Cyril have joined the Mercedes Club, which involves weekend jaunts out in their stylish cars for picnics and bubbles. Since I have also been invited to join them, I have had to warn the horse and kayak fraternity that I may not always be available. How do you think I would rather spend a Sunday?

I had a narrow escape recently. I keep a night light on in my open walk-in wardrobe, between my bedroom and bathroom. The other night I was sitting up in bed watching the television, when I noticed that the bulb had gone out. I got up and took it out of its socket thinking I might be able to repair it! Big mistake for one who knows nothing about electrics! I caught hold of something I shouldn't have and was knocked backwards. Rather shell shocked, I found the palm of my hand was completely covered with soot and I also had a slight burn. At the same time the television popped and went off. When I recovered from the shock I realised how stupid I had been since everything was still connected to the mains! I then started worrying and felt I couldn't go to sleep in case something, due to my stupidity, could cause a fire during the night. I considered sending for the fire brigade, but wasn't sure it would warrant a visit. So, although I prefer not to call on Jan and Andrew too often, I decided that the occasion was serious enough to do so.

What I didn't know was that they were entertaining and when Jan answered the phone I could tell by her voice, which was unusually jolly, that she had obviously been imbibing. I apologised for the intrusion and told her what had happened. In her 'jolly' state she announced to the gathered company that her mother had had a 'crisis' – her TV had gone off! Great gales of laughter from the other end.

Then Andrew came on the line to hear what had happened and again announced to the gathering that they, meaning Jan and he, were 'nearly rich just now.' Even I couldn't help but laugh about that comment knowing that they might get a shock when the time comes. Just because I know how to 'put on the style', it doesn't mean that I'm loaded!

Of course, they came round to see that I was all right and without a doubt I have learnt my lesson. In spite of the fact that I feel I have become a big girl doing all sorts of tasks around the house since I have lived by myself, I am very much aware of the dangers. Perhaps I do need another male around, if only to carry the suitcases!

In spite of my protests that I never wanted anyone to love again since I could not bare the pain of loss, and my intention to remain by myself forever to try to enjoy my time of utter freedom – I find that things have vastly altered. This is the way it came about.

A LEAP INTO THE UNKNOWN

Jan was out riding her horse when she rang me to say that she had found the tiniest little kitten, starved and half frozen to death, who would surely die within the next few hours – and could she bring it home to me? (She not being able to have it herself due to her own cat, who rules the roost). I pleaded with her not to do this to me; I just couldn't face commitment and possibly pain again. She assured me that if only she could bring it home, I could restore it to health and then she would then deliver it to the Cats Protection people. One week and $300 later (£100 sterling), I have the dearest little kitten who owns his own feeding bowls, filled with the best special kitten foods that money can buy; he has a little padded house to sleep in, he has a sheepskin rug to stand on should he venture out, he has a sort of carpet-covered pole on which to scratch, he has a dangly thing that he can hit with his little paw and he has a couple of stuffed mice to kick around. He has visited the vet who has told me my kitten is only eight weeks old and given the little darling any jab he might need – at a price, of course. I have something really neurotic to confess. I simply wanted his birth date confirmed, so I took him to another vet for a second opinion and confirmation!

He will have to have a little leather collar with his name and telephone number on it, but at present I can't seem to find what I want for him, which will have to be diamante-studded. I want the locals (cats, of course) to know he is in training to be a very discerning gentleman full of style. He purrs like a little motor each time I cuddle him and he looks up at me with the most endearing eyes. He is now my cat, but he calls the shots. As Jan pointed out when it was far too late for me to see sense, 'Dogs have owners, cats have staff!'

Next thing was to think of a name for him. I toyed with Liberty, since he was found wandering all alone, but thought it might possibly be shortened to Libby, which wouldn't suit a male cat. After much serious consideration and since I only want the best for him, I knew what name he was to answer to. So the next time Jan came round and asked me what I was going to call him, I announced that I had decided to call him after the gentleman who had given me the most pleasure in my life. Naturally, her ears pricked up and she waited with baited breath to hear who that could possibly be.

He is named after that grand old Edwardian gentleman who gave us all those wonderfully regal tunes that we love to sing in honour of our country – Sir Edward Elgar! My dearest dear is called Elgar and I love him to bits.

18

It is still winter here and it's been, on average, six below zero for the past two weeks. I have been hibernating, mainly staying indoors reading, listening to music and cuddling my little darling!

When I first arrived in NZ and had so much to explore and to sort out my new life, to make a new home, to learn, everybody said how interesting my emails home were, so full of news compared with theirs. I think I have reached a stage where the pace of life has slowed down. Finally, after two and a half years, I am as happy as I can be with my new existence and life seems to be ticking over quite nicely with my monthly soirees, which give me great pleasure, plus other entertainments so frequent and varied. Best of all, the delight and comfort of my little furry friend.

One of my grandsons, Wes, came to spend a week with me and apart from the usual drag round the shopping malls, eating out, eating in (takeaways!) and endless games of cards, we had a real adventure.

In the surrounding fields very near to me is a 'heritage village', where a collection of original dwellings built by the early settlers has been gathered together. They have added a complete early Maori settlement in the same vicinity, run by the same firm as the one I visited in Rotarua. Jan, Wes and I went along to investigate and it proved to be just as fascinating an evening as the one I had been so delighted with before.

Maori actors took us back in history to pre-settler days, through the trauma of the changes that Captain Cook brought. We were lead through fields, across rivers and were guided through the village, experiencing their way of living. They did a re-enactment of a battle, fighting on foot and also on horseback – really impressive. The Maoris have a war-like reputation and tribal feuding still breaks out today.

We eventually landed in a large entertainment room for the excellent singing and dancing and a fabulous dinner – a real banquet. My only regret was that I didn't take my camera. I shall have to go again!

Sir Edward Elgar has truly wormed his way into my affections and taken over the house. I talk to Elgar like Mr Bean used to talk to his little brown bear, asking it for advice and approval.

He follows me everywhere and when I come down in the morning or come home, he immediately wants to be picked up and sits on the veranda that my boobs supply, snuggles into my neck and purrs like a little motorbike. Although I ban him from my bedroom since I must have somewhere to call my own, he seems to understand and it makes him more determined to go in. A few days ago he cunningly sneaked in and hid from me. I could clearly see by the little mound his body made that he was hiding under the satin counterpane. I called his name, but he kept perfectly still, thinking that I couldn't see him hiding there! Whenever I go out, I leave classical music playing to enhance his taste and give him intellectual stimulation.

He continues to be an expense. Apart from the special kitten food, he has a vast selection of stimulating toys and has been back to the vet for a further check-up. I had to have the burglar alarm modified due to the extra movement around the house when it's switched on. Never mind, he is my little darling and as long as he continues to use his 'dirt box', he stays!

The weather is changing again and spring is here. Hagley Park, in the middle of Christchurch (so big that it actually has a golf course in it) is awash with daffodils, and yet the Southern Alps, which run all the way down the South Island, are crisp with sparkling snow, so, lucky me, I get two diverse views as I drive into town.

'Spring is a time when youth dreams and old age remembers.' (Unknown.)

The mountains that surround my house are full of ewes and their lambs so I constantly hear the surprisingly noisy bleating of the lambs calling for their mothers. Just recently there was an article in the local newspaper about locals who are proving to be rather a nuisance. They are interfering with the natural process of things by going about trying to place the lambs with their mothers, and when not successful, actually picking them up and taking them to the RSPCA, or even taking them home and then ringing the rangers. I find this amazing as even a person like me who is totally unused to farming life wouldn't consider doing this. Surely one has to let nature take its course in these matters? As the nursery rhyme says; 'Leave them alone and they will come home, dragging their tails behind them.'

Living here, I get the waves of the Pacific Ocean crashing in from one direction and at the same time hear the bleating of the lambs from another!

Even though I have been here two and a half years now, I am still discovering the delights of Christchurch. We are in the middle of a spring festival, which I seem to have missed before. Like all activities that take place here, it's absolutely wonderful. All month long there are superb arts event including literature, opera, the symphony orchestra, individual concerts, choral, jazz, street entertainment – everything you could possibly think of.

I had heard that a pavilion had been built in Cathedral Square and had automatically assumed that it would be the usual run-of-the-mill temporary construction. But no! This was fantastic and I was duly impressed. It was the usual pavilion-type shape, but it had a wood block floor; ornate, leaded light windows surrounding the outer structure; alcoves with tables and chairs, divided by trellis work; mirrored glass pillars around the centre 'ballroom' area, where a huge chandelier of tulip-shaped bulbs hung over the centre, plus tulip bulb wall fittings were placed around the outer sides. Delightful refreshments were served to guests at the events. I imagined it looked stunning at night.

Now for more news of the most important thing of my life – Sir Edward Elgar.

To my surprise, I am turning into a sweet little old granny who happily sits in her chair and cuddles her precious pussycat whenever she can. I am totally and utterly smitten with him, although the pleasure of his company has been quite an expense to me. Apart from the fact that he has everything he could possibly desire plus regular health checks, he has developed a cold and needed to have antibiotic treatment. The vet thinks that, due to his poor start in life, he might have suffered lung damage. I thought something was wrong because as I clasped him to my breast, his purring started to sound like an old man's heavy breathing! I hope it improves! In addition to that, he had his claws clipped. They were so long, I didn't know whether to paint them or have them manicured and he was scratching me to pieces. In fact, my hands were so scratched that some kind gentleman remarked on it and was quite surprised when I said, 'You ought to see my thighs!'

It was wonderful being married to my own personal doctor, but now perhaps I should be on the look out for a vet as a possible future husband!

Sir Edward Elgar has shown how much he loves me and as he follows me from room to room and gambols around my feet, I have to walk around indoors as though I am skiing. This being because I have trodden on him several times and actually sat on him once – and with my bottom it wasn't a pleasant experience for him, poor little thing!

He totally trusts me and, surrendering himself to me, he lays on his back with all four paws in the air as I stroke his tummy. It appears to be an orgasmic experience for him, which reminds me, I must get his tackle fixed before much longer! I don't want a full orchestra of little Elgars overrunning the house! He loves me so much that he even licks my face – I know I sound sick, but I must confess I used to enjoy it and find it comforting. It drastically changed when I observed him cleaning himself. It's amazing the places his little tongue can reach and I suddenly don't want it on my face anymore.

As a result of all this, I have been through a vast change in my life; I have slipped into a totally different persona altogether. No more high life, fancy clothes, jewels, furs, feathers, audience adoration, etc. I have, at last, thanks to the love of a little fluffy animal, accepted what fate has decreed will be my future. I'm not alone anymore. I have my Elgar. Now, after all that I appear to have given up, you will be pleased to know that I still have the wicked sense of humour that used to shock and delight Colin. I lay in the bath, every morning, dreaming up 'pussy' jokes to shock the locals. Here are a few I have come up with so far and I must say, my reminiscences of Mrs Slocombe from *Are You Being Served?* have helped tremendously. So here goes:

1. 'If my pussy doesn't get seen to before 10 p.m. I'm up all night stroking it';
2. 'Everybody, unanimously, enjoys stroking my little furry pussy';
3. 'A thought came to me the other day. If I continue spending money at this rate, I'll have to send my pussy out to work';
4. 'My pussy loves to be tickled; in fact, it gets quite excited';
5. 'I accidentally sprayed my pussy with perfume the other day. It was dreadful – I had all the tom cats in the area throwing themselves at my cat flap all night'.

I feel sure far more will surface – it just needs more hot water and bubbles to get the imagination flowing!

As I look around at the house and garden, in spite of all my reticence, I must admit that I am beginning to feel very satisfied with it all – and even settled! I think I have a really pleasant existence now and I am gradually experiencing a slow but sure love affair with Christchurch. I attend at least two events each week and am enjoying all sorts of different activities. I also have my wonderful Sumner Soiree group of ladies who have given me such purpose. Even if there is nothing 'official' to attend, we still meet for the occasional lunch. In fact, one of the husbands has dubbed his wife 'Lady Lunchalot', which I thought most appropriate.

The Christchurch Symphony Orchestra had a world-famous pianist as a guest artist and arranged a special evening for the Friends of the Orchestra (of which I am one) to meet him. It transpired to be a most delightful evening. We gathered in the Christchurch Club where he spoke about his training, travelling and music in general and then he played a few pieces for us.

Since there were only about forty of us, it was very intimate and as I sat watching him at the piano, I thought how reminiscent it was of the Victorian soirees. I really wished Colin could have been there with me. I know for sure he would, like me, have been enthralled by it all. It was rounded off very nicely with delicious canapés and glasses of wine. All very civilised.

Another grand occasion was in a titled lady's house. How the other half live! That too was by invitation of the CCSO. It was a lunchtime event and the house and garden were stunning. The garden looked manicured to within an inch of its life, everything was so perfect. We sat down to a wonderful lunch with the sweet music of a solo flautist and then a violinist drifting gently over the proceedings. Another occasion that Colin would have loved. I can't help feeling tinges of guilt at enjoying so much that he would have enjoyed, when he is not here.

I'm sorry and ashamed to say my enthusiasm at joining the local gym didn't last! It became far too dispiriting for me. All that huffing and puffing when my heart wasn't truly in it. In fact, I got totally fed-up with the enthusiasm of those 'jolly hockey sticks' types, so I left. I think what made me finally realise that it just wasn't me was when I became more interested in the delights of the bar at the end of each session. Sorry!

As NZ is a nation of sports-orientated people and everyone is so fit, it tends to make someone like me who sits around reading, listening to music or watching DVDs feel like a little pudding, which I readily admit I am. Having already tried yoga and the gym unsuccessfully, I thought I ought to have a go at pilates.

I enrolled for six weeks of private lessons, thinking it would be more helpful in 'breaking me in'. Big mistake. With only me to concentrate on, the instructor ensured that I worked hard and made good progress, which presented rather a strain on me. I much prefer to loiter at the back of a hall pretending to work. I have tentatively tried to express that to her and perhaps admit that I don't seem to be able to grasp the point of it all, but now, instead of gently letting me go, she is suggesting that I go Nordic walking with her group.

Nordic walking – what the hell is that? I'll tell you what it is. You have to get all togged up in anoraks, scarves and gloves and wear the most unfashionable walking boots. You then grasp two poles, which look like ski thingys, and venture forth with other health-seeking souls in what looks like a mixture of walking and skiing. I don't doubt we will all look like total 'wallys'!

I haven't got the nerve to say I just don't want to do it, so I'll just have to go to my first trial session, hoping that no-one I know spots me progressing along the beach looking like I am trying to walk on the moon! Why, oh why, do I get myself in these situations? Why can't I just admit to being me?

I've worked out that since we have been on such intimate terms during the pilates lessons, the only way I can let the instructor know without disappointing her too much is to say that I am off to the UK for a long holiday, which could be true, eventually. Well, it's not a complete lie and she won't know that, will she?

The only problem is that I will just have to go about the village disguised in a raincoat, hat, moustache and thick black-rimmed glasses until she forgets me!

My little dearest pussycat continues to bring me great joy and, as the weeks progress, is becoming a wonderful companion. He is still only four and a half months old, so acts like a baby. He wants to play with me all the time and he is sitting on my shoulder, tapping my cheek, as I write! He shoots everywhere as though he has been blasted from a cannon and having an open plan house, he makes a tremendous noise scampering up and down stairs, jumping on and off the furniture and generally throwing himself all over the place. Everybody tells me he will calm down when he has visited the vet – poor thing.

I still won't allow him in my bedroom. The only problem is that he wakes up at 5 a.m. sharp and sits outside my bedroom door crying until I let him in. He then proceeds to jump all over me while I am trying to snatch those last few cosy minutes of warmth in bed before surfacing. Of course, being so fresh in the morning, he tends to be rather frisky and keeps trying to rout me out. He even jumps on my head!

NZ television is currently showing a serial about *The Hound of the Baskervilles* and during the introduction they show a horrible paw, clawing at the window. Even though I try to keep my head well under the covers, if I tentatively peep out I am faced with a similar paw stretching menacingly towards me. I hurriedly retract my poor head before it is seriously attacked.

Jan says that she is going to leave a door or window open so that he runs away and gets lost. She thinks I love him more than her! She also informed me that when I go to that great Orchestral Concert in the sky and she is left to adopt him, he'll get a shock when he faces 'real life' instead of all the pampering he gets now. I decided it was her that would get the shock and I told her that I had been to a solicitor and changed my will in favour of him. He not only inherits the house, but has his own housekeeper as well.

Time for some pussy jokes I think as per 'Mrs Slocombe'.
1. 'I've got a whole row of silver cups for my pussy. It wins a prize every time I show it';
2. 'My poor pussy had to have some teeth out. It doesn't seem to mind too much, it just has to suck harder';
3. 'I'm so worried about going away from home. I don't know how my pussy will take to sleeping in a strange bed!';
4. 'I am getting so worried – the gardener only has to ring the bell and my pussy's hair stands on end.'

I was speaking to someone the other day and they told me that you really can give your pussycat a message that he will understand

and respond to. Apparently, if you open your mouth wide and, at the same time, blink slowly, it inspires great feelings of love and friendship. This was told to me in all seriousness, so I often try it when he looks up at me. In all honestly, I can't report any great change, except to say my mouth and eyes are beginning to ache. I must be sure not to let Jan catch me doing this exercise or she really will begin to worry!

I had a wonderful weekend at Jan and Andrew's place in Picton. This is not for them to live in, but an investment and a means of making money with passing tourists who want luxury accommodation. They have bought a motor boat for their own use whenever they avail themselves of the apartment.

The only problem with this trip was that I had to put Elgar into a cattery. I took the poor little soul along and was not at all happy about it. The place itself was good and all the cats had their own little rooms, but there was a radio playing with the type of music that Elgar simply isn't used to and it rather disturbed me, considering he is only used to Chopin and such.

I have had proof that he is susceptible to music – I put Maria Callas on and the poor little soul quickly ran under the sideboard and wouldn't come out until I stopped playing the CD. Anyway, back at the cattery. Not wanting to appear totally mad, I just had to leave him to face the music, knowing for sure I couldn't have lived with it for four whole days. The owners assured me that the cats found music comforting. I held back from saying that my cat, even though he couldn't stomach the drama of Maria Callas, had a more discerning taste!

When we got to Picton, the weather was kind to us so we went out in the boat visiting the various coves around the harbour and it made a great change. When Jan and Andrew were sitting supping wine in the gardens of a pub on the Norfolk Broads many years ago, a cabin cruiser passed by with a couple in the front and an old granny sitting in the back. Jan told me that at that time Andrew turned to her and scornfully said, 'That's you, me and your mother in the future!' He had no idea that it would ever come to pass.

Now Jan is in fits of laughter about it coming true and having me parked in the back like a *grande dame*, encroaching on all their pleasure!

On the second day we travelled around the vineyards of the famous Blenheim area. These vineyards not only have tastings but scrumptious restaurants. We sampled absolutely everything and rolled home hating ourselves for imbibing and throwing all caution to the wind, gorging on all the fancy dishes offered to us.

I have become so attached to Sir Edward that I was really pleased when we started the journey home. The first thing I did on arriving was to go to the cattery and collect him. Oh, how comforting it was. The moment he saw me and I picked him up, he snuggled his head into my neck and purred like a little motorbike engine, and when I actually brought him home it was as though he was stuck to my shoe. I tried to do the unpacking, but could hardly move because of him. He really is a little darling and brings me so much joy and comfort. And, what's more, I was so pleased to find that he didn't appear too traumatised by the awful music he had been subjected to.

19

SOS! I've just experienced my second earthquake and it was pretty scary! It centred in Hanmer, where the roads were described as 'rolling'! It was about 8.15 a.m. and I was doing my usual thing of checking the computer for emails from home. There was a tremendous bang and, if I didn't have a high brick wall at the front and the garden wasn't so big, I really would have thought that a huge lorry had smashed into the house at top speed. I went to investigate but after looking around and finding nothing unusual and being totally unaware of what had happened, I just got on with my normal activities.

It wasn't until much later in the day that I heard the reports on the news. In spite of damage, amazingly no-one had been hurt. It amazed me that the effects could be felt so far away, Hanmer being 140 km north of Christchurch.

The weather is brighter and poor little Elgar looks longingly out of the French windows down into the garden, obviously yearning for his freedom. Unfortunately, he just has to wait until he visits the vet for the big operation and I might add here that it seems to be quite necessary now, since he appears to have become rather keen on the teddy bear I have on my bed.

I fancied a dose of Shakespeare the other day and put on a DVD of *A Midsummer Night's Dream*. At the time he was sitting on my lap but when he noticed that it was set in woodland, he jumped off my lap, scampered across the floor, jumped up onto the television table and sat directly in front of the screen watching with great intent! Even occasionally, touching the greenery of the Forest of Arden with his little paw.

I recently enjoyed a very interesting evening organised by the Symphony Orchestra called 'I Love Paris'. It began with a concert of music and songs associated with France, ending with the Can Can performed with great gusto. It was all most entertaining and afterwards we were invited to dinner with the orchestra. When we walked into the dining room, it was utterly amazing. It really looked like a street in France with models of the Arc de Triumph, the Eiffel Tower and the Metro, draped with fairy lights. The invitation suggested that we all come dressed up suitably attired in fishnet stockings, feather boas, berets etc. so this helped create an electric atmosphere and we all had great fun. It was magical!

The French cuisine and wines went down very nicely, as we were serenaded by a cabaret artist. I really felt happy that evening, which was an extra bonus and a wonderful feeling for me, because it seems to have taken ages since Colin went for the overwhelming misery to subside.

The wonderful Pavarotti passed away recently – he certainly gave so much to this world and I feel sure that many who would not have considered opera before must think of him with gratitude for introducing them to this wonderful art form. As it happened, I was booked to do one of my Sumner Soirees the week his death was announced, so naturally decided to dedicate the event to him.

I set up a little altar with two pictures of him, a small vase of flowers and his customary large white handkerchief. We lit a huge candle which burnt throughout the afternoon as we sat and watched snippets from DVDs that I had collected of him in performance over the years.

The most exciting and poignant point for us was when he was joined by the Three Tenors and his enjoyment, enthusiasm and love for his art and others was so obvious. All of us senior ladies were so inspired that we yelled out 'We love you, Pavarotti' and by the end we felt we had paid our respects to the great man in as grand a way as possible.

Now we are swiftly approaching the end of another year, bringing with it the predictable analysis of what has been achieved.

'As the wheel of the decades turn, so do a person's needs, desire and takes.' (Unknown.)

'Each of us does, in effect, strike a series of deals or compromises between the want and longings of the inner self, and an outer environment that offers certain possibilities and sets certain limitation.' (Maggie Scarf.)

This year I seem to be more confused than ever. I still can't let go of the life I've known. I still yearn for what I had in England – Colin and our home and all the other things that gave purpose to our existence. I ponder on my favourite places on earth and still come up with Stratford upon Avon and the Cotswolds, Aldeburgh, Rye and Italy. These are places where Colin and I enjoyed visiting and felt truly happy.

I constantly think about my old friends and the times we had together. I think about all the preparation that went into producing my little entertainments and feel a huge gap in my life without all that.

'Ever has it been that love knows not its own depth until the hour of separation.' (Kahlil Gibran.)

I now live the comfortable life of a retired lady, in a lovely house, in a delightful seaside area near a major town which, apart from being beautifully situated with the River Avon wending its weary way throughout, has many surprising and interesting events staged to stimulate the intellectual taste buds. All this, in a country that is still reasonably unspoilt by the rapid progress of the world. I now have a new set of lovely friends too. People that really seem to enjoy my company, as I do theirs. Lastly, the cherry on the cake must be my little furry companion, Sir Edward Elgar.

I try to weigh it all up hoping to come to the conclusion that I am better off where I am, in a very beautiful country and near my two girls, but after being here nearly three years now I don't feel completely settled and contented.

   Is it like this with all ex-pats? I know for sure that I appreciate all I have and do and it's not as though I'm terribly unhappy because I know full well that I am enjoying my new life in many ways. Where is the missing link? Why can't I feel totally settled? Here is a poem I recently found, which seems to pretty much sum it all up:

> If you plan to leave my shores
> Do it when you're very young.
> Leave before your memory stores
> Knowledge of your mother tongue.
> Leave before you call me 'home'
> And before your heart is given
> Because, if after that you roam,
> Then forever you are riven.
>
> Though your eyes may seek and find
> Wondrous sights on land and sea
> You will always find your mind
> Turning homeward, back to me
> You will hunger, you will thirst,
> You will suffer all your days,
> Yearning for what you knew first,
> English folk and English ways.
>
> English lanes with hedges high
> English gardens all in bloom
> English earth and English sky,
> English fields, and English coomb.
> English habits, eyes that smile,
> English jokes I think are funny,
> English clothing worn with style.
> English weather, damp or sunny.

A LEAP INTO THE UNKNOWN

And in your rememberings,
Let the pride blot out the pain.
Pride in England's kings and queens,
Pride in speaking England's name.
Pride in all that made me great,
Pride in my illustrious past.
Pride in that I played the game
And shall until the very last.

(Unknown.)

Oh dear – will I ever be able to let go?

Alfred and Barbara have recently paid me a visit and together we had a little holiday in Jan and Andrew's magnificent apartment in Picton. Everything was just about as perfect as could be until ... all hell broke loose. This is how we came to have a real adventure.

Deep in slumber one night, we were rudely awaken by a tremendous alarm and a stern voice urgently announcing, 'Evacuate the building from your nearest fire exit. Evacuate the building from your nearest fire exit.' Over and over again. As you can imagine, pandemonium broke out!

All three of us dithering old age pensioners immediately adopted a very sensible stance – I don't think! Poor dear Barbara is registered blind, so Alfred and I were vying to help her out. She, being somewhat bossy, was trying to sort us out! This resulted in a lot of confusion and bumping into each other.

Naturally, people in this situation can be forgiven for grabbing the nearest and dearest thing to them. Barbara grabbed her knickers, I grabbed my wig and Alfred, the old skinflint, grabbed his wallet! That was just the start of the pantomime that was about to follow. Unable to see anything, we headed for the lift but realised that not only might it be out of order, but that it could be hazardous, so we groped our way in search of the stairs. With no light and being totally unfamiliar with our surroundings, we tried with great trepidation to negotiate our descent. As it happened, Barbara proved to be the best leader since she was so familiar with the dark and seemed to have a heightened sense of touch – so it became a case of the blind leading the blind.

To the continual blast of the Klaxon fire alarm and the urgent announcement, we eventually burst forth into the car park. Looking around, it was almost comforting to find everyone else tussle-haired and bleary-eyed, in their nightclothes too (which were on the whole well worn and faded). All except a young couple who seemed to have no nightclothes and had wrapped themselves in sheets.

Much to my delight, I seemed to be the only stylish figure there, dressed in my beautiful satin leopard-print pyjamas with my immaculately groomed blonde hair. Perhaps you can imagine how deflated I felt when Alfred, in his loud theatrical voice asked, 'Did you manage to get your teeth in, Marie?' I hadn't even given them a thought.

At that moment Barbara, who was wearing garish Cinderella slippers and dressed in her short 'baby-doll' nightdress (circa 1960 by the look of it) announced that she was feeling the draft and needed to put her knickers on. While perched on one leg, shakily attempting to scramble into them, I noticed a young man observing the scene with great glee and trying to control his gurgling laughter.

I must say that a rotund seventy-plus lady wearing Cinderella slippers, struggling into bright scarlet knickers, is not a pretty sight and I felt obliged to say so to him. That, of course, opened the floodgates of his suppressed glee and, with great relief, he collapsed into gales of laughter.

Having managed, with great huffing and puffing, to scramble into her outrageous knickers, she then realised that she needed to go to the loo. Alfred led her away to a private corner where she could freely relieve herself. Unfortunately, both were totally unaware that the terra firma had quite a severe rake which caused her wee to gush steamingly towards the bare and slippered feet of the assembled crowd!

After witnessing the relief of Barbara's flow, Alfred realised that he too wanted to go. Having adopted the usual manly stance and relaxing well into a wonderful feeling of relief, he was horrified to see enquiring faces peering through his chosen wall, which, if fact, was a dense metal fence. Of course, once the flow had started, he found it impossible to stop, so holding his wizened and shrivelled member and yet continuing the flow, he nonchalantly strolled off, only to be faced with yet another group of escapees coming from a different direction.

Although upset with a mixture of fear and the chill night air, the assembled crowd started to tentatively chat to each other, when suddenly someone called to the crowd, 'Oh look! There's poor Mr Lawrence!' Everyone turned around to see a very shaky old gentleman with two sticks, wobbling unsteadily down the stairs. Although it was a pitiful sight, we really couldn't control our nervous laughter.

With the siren continuing to blast away and the ceaseless warning from the monotonous voice, I couldn't help wondering if this could be considered as slightly reminiscent of the Blitz in London. Of course, our danger was very much less but nevertheless seemed quite a real threat to the motley group of people shaken from their cosy slumbers.

Eventually, we were permitted to return to the building, so zombie-like we staggered back to the sanctuary of our apartment. Upon returning, we couldn't resist leaning over the balcony to see the spectacular sight of the two fire engines with their flashing lights. Forgetting our recent traumas and like American or Japanese tourists, we grabbed our cameras to capture the reality of the moment for prosperity. After all the excitement and having comforted ourselves with a hot drink, we all agreed as we dashed to our respective loos that fire scares were a wonderful remedy for constipation.

Arising sleepily the following morning, Barbara and I mulled over the possibility of being rescued and manhandled by a big burly young fireman, but Alfred quickly dispelled our fantasies by assuring us that surely none would consider us worth saving!

Entering the lift on our way out for the day, we met one of the other inhabitants and started exchanging stories of the previous night. Alfred confessed to having smoke in his eyes and I to actually smelling smoke. Both ridiculous, of course, since there had been no fire. The gentleman said that he too was puzzled since it wasn't apparent that any water had been used by the fire brigade and yet he had actually experienced wet feet! Being of a mature age and worldly wise, we managed to control our inner mirth and steered the conversation towards the weather and how grateful we were to be able to look forward to another day.

Another event at Christchurch Town Hall was the NZ Symphony Orchestra offering their version of 'The Last Night of the Proms' – and I must admit it was really very good. The programme was predominately Gilbert and Sullivan and the orchestra was joined by professional opera singers which gave more colour to the occasion, ending end with the customary 'Rule Britannia' and 'Land of Hope and Glory'. It truly was a most enjoyable and rousing evening, so rousing in fact, that I wept all the way home. I miss England so much, especially dressing up as Britannia and doing my stuff – I told Sir Edward Elgar so when I arrived home and hugged him tight and covered him in wet, tearful kisses.

This brings me very nicely to the love of my life, my dear little pussycat. I love him so much and if he goes and gets run over – well, I'll never speak to him again!

He has now had the 'operation', poor thing. Never mind, we all have to face these things in life. Anyway, I considered that after five months indoors with only me for company, it was only fair for him to see the big outside world at last, especially after witnessing his great interest in *A Midsummer Night's Dream*. I gently took him in my arms, and for the first time ever, out to the garden.

We walked around and I told him all about the garden and how it was the special domain that we shared with each other. When I put him down, it was so fascinating just to stand back and watch him. He didn't immediately run away, but tentatively investigated all around him, sniffing, patting and poking at things, and even jumping lamb-like over little bushes. Naturally, it wasn't long before he got the hang of things and I just had to watch him disappear into the bushes hoping and praying that he would find his way home.

Every time he goes out, he continually rushes back in to check where I am. I find this utterly astounding. One day I took particular note of it. He was out and about for approximately two hours and during that time he rushed back in eight times, found where I was in the house, meowed at me and simply turned and rushed back out again. It was as if he was checking on me. Actions speak louder than words, they say. How nice to be needed.

'The mind should be like a camera – loaded with appreciation, ready to capture in full color and in perfect focus the essence of each beautiful moment.' (Jim Beggs.)

I have faced a lot of changes these last four years and I must admit that most of the time fate has been very kind to me, especially bringing this little darling into my life. I am so very grateful for him.

20

Christmas has come and gone again and, here we are, starting a New Year with all the good intentions and promises that could make life perfect. I understand that, apart from anything else, many slimming regimes are undertaken with great determination, followed by the devastating disappointment of failure. Why, oh why, can't a crisp, juicy apple be as enticing as a delicious glass of chilled wine, plus the customary nibbles that accompany it?

'It only takes one person to change your life – you!' (Ruth Casey.)

Christmas has been good for me this year. Apart from the usual public Christmas entertainments, I have been inundated with invitations to dinner parties, cocktail parties and such, for which I have been exceedingly grateful. Unaware that one has to book early for places at the cattery, I left it too late to place Sir Edward Elgar and therefore was unable to fly to Wellington to be with the family. As it happened, things panned out very nicely. All the family came and filled the house here instead! The weather was good, bright, hot and sunny and time was spent in the garden or at the beach. Having three teenage grandsons, I wanted to prise them away from the computer screen and see them engaged in something more active. One cannot deny the marvel of computers, but I they seem disastrous for normal family interaction.

I had what I thought was the brilliant idea of a water fight in the garden. I bought copious amounts of water balloons and bombs, wrapped them up as Christmas gifts and waited for the response – and I certainly wasn't disappointed.

When the boys unwrapped their unlikely gifts, their first reaction was of utter bewilderment, but it wasn't too long before screams of surprise and delight echoed through the neighbourhood as they started hurling the filled bombs at each other. I had also bought a couple of water pistols in the hope that the adults would join in but the enthusiasm was so great that two garden hoses were also soon in action. It really was a fun afternoon that worked up a keen appetite for the Christmas dinner.

Just before Christmas, the local pet shop had a huge banner inviting shoppers to have a picture taken of their pet with Santa. I immediately saw this as a chance to have some more fun with Jan and develop the idea that I now hold my little cat in as much regard as I would a human person. I told her that I had discussed it with Sir Edward. Obviously, he didn't actually speak to me, but made it quite clear to me that he considered it to be rather tasteless. However, he would consider having a photograph taken with me, his beloved companion, and possibly printed as a Christmas card.

No sooner had the family left for home in Wellington, than I had more visitors. My friends Alfred and Barbara, who had theatrical friends of their own visiting from Spain, rang to ask if they could all visit me.

Although feeling somewhat weary after such an active Christmas, I was pleased to welcome them. What fun it all was! The assembled group of us old people talking about the old times 'treading the boards'. I'm sure that, on overhearing us, any younger person could never have pictured us as young, vibrant and, may I say, even good-looking. As I always say, it's better to be a 'has been' than a 'never was'!

Nevertheless I couldn't help agreeing with Victor Borge who said; 'Santa Claus has the right idea. Visit people only once a year.'

With all the visitors over and done, I was rather glad of a rest and to get back into the old routine.

I had a very pleasant evening when Jan came round with a group of her friends and played boules in the garden, accompanied of course with nibbles and plentiful wine! And it's good to see some activity in the garden.

A friend invited me to go for a walk and I was so surprised to be taken through 'real bush' (forest to us Brits!) in the very centre of Christchurch. One of the first immigrants from England had fortuitously decided that rather than cultivate his piece of land, he would leave it exactly how he had found it. It was not only a wonderful piece of natural history but a magical place which almost seemed 'spiritual'. I was utterly spellbound and certainly intend to take any other visitors I might have in the future to this miraculously saved remnant of history. I simply had no idea it was there and feel delighted to list it in my records for future visitors. It was quite incredible.

During a routine 'well woman' check-up, it was discovered that I have exceedingly high cholesterol. This caused quite a fuss but after a consultation at the hospital and medication, I am now within the normal range. Unfortunately something else has come to light, which I can't believe.

Quite recently, when I returned to the hospital for a check-up, I was asked to take a record with me of all that I had consumed during the preceding week. During the consultation, the professor said how pleased he was that such a swift change had occurred since the last consultation. With medication, the cholesterol appeared to be well under control, but the tests had revealed something else which needed to be addressed. He needed to investigate my eating regime. As he commented, I start the day very sensibly with a bowl of porridge, but from that point on, it appears that I am at a perpetual cocktail party consisting of wine and nibbles! Well, we both had a laugh about it but I felt obliged to point out that I have always hated cooking and since I live alone, there doesn't seem to be any point in it all, plus I couldn't see what was lacking in toasted sandwiches, salad and fruit etc. with a few packets of crisps, nuts and other odds and ends thrown in!

I must confess the next revelation to come did rather shock me. He said that the results of the blood test had shown that I was undernourished and suffering from malnutrition! I really couldn't believe such a thing and said how astounded I was and asked him if he would like to inspect my tummy, bottom and thighs!

In addition to the cholesterol treatment, I am now on a special programme to build up my vitamin intake and with strict instructions to 'eat properly'. He told me that a cardiologist friend had always offered this advice, 'If it tastes good, spit it out!'

Because I find it all rather amusing, I have been playfully lowering my head on my friends' chests and telling them of my sorrowful state and, as a result of this, they have been bringing me samples of their wonderful home cooking. One friend even arrived with a carrier full of frozen dinners! I am exceedingly indebted, but what a laugh!

'Be careful about reading health books. You may die of a misprint.' (Mark Twain.)

I have purchased a slow cooker; I have been buying meat and fish, plus loads of vegetables and have been letting it do its magic all day long. The annoying thing about all this is that, although I really am eating sensibly and drinking very little wine (only when people visit, just to be sociable) and have been consuming absolutely no rubbishy nibbles at all, I have put on more weight!

'One should eat to live, not live to eat.' (Molière.)

I really have started to think sensibly about keeping fit. It really is ridiculous that I live by the seaside and hardly ever go to the beach, so I now take myself off for a walk along the promenade occasionally and, I'm pleased to say, several of my friends have been driving out to join me.

I am still suffering from denture problems. Having paid mega bucks for two sets of dentures from two different operatives, neither of them are comfortable, even after returning several times to have them refitted. In conclusion, I have no intention of continually returning for more treatment. I have now located a place in each of the sets that rubs and hurts, so, as the soreness develops, I simply chop and change from one set to the other. All this seemed to work reasonably well until I rethought the scenario and decided that I really ought to sort it out and went to a new man. On inspection, he announced that I was wearing a set of dentures that were not a match (what a surprise!) and he could provide me with a new set ... at which point I headed for the door in a cloud of dust!

One of my friends is an official tour guide around Christchurch, so I decided to join one of his tours myself. It was absolutely fascinating and has left me full of enthusiasm, so much so that it didn't take much persuading for me to agree to train to be a guide myself. Most of the guides appear to be retired teachers and they think that I would be really suited to the job. Apparently, the training is quite involved with tests etc. but I am looking forward to it.

My Sumner Soirees are still proving to be very successful and there is even a waiting list of people who want to join. It has been suggested that I start another at the Christchurch Club where many more could attend, but I am reluctant to do that because I could see it developing into real 'work' again. In any case, I think the charm about it all is the way it is conducted, in my own home.

A group of approximately ten regulars arrive once a month, laden with home-made goodies, we all share a wonderful lunch together, then watch whatever intellectual and classical entertainment I have planned. My plan is to do a different area each month – grand opera, operetta, Gilbert and Sullivan, literature (Shakespeare, Dickens etc.), art, architecture, history and so on.

This month, I showed them a wonderful DVD about Bernini, the highly gifted Italian artist, architect and sculptor of the Renaissance. It is a particularly stimulating time for me and I just love sharing all the fantastic videos and DVDs that I have collected over the years with this set of wonderful friends. It's something I look forward to tremendously every month ... and I get to eat 'real' food!

The group of ladies are so enthusiastic that I suggested we had a flappers' garden party where we would all dress up in the style of the roaring twenties and even allow the husbands to come. One of the husbands came early and erected the gazebos in the garden for shade, while I set up tables with crisp white tablecloths in preparation for the ladies laden with all sorts of goodies to arrive. To the strains of Charleston music, we even managed a civilised game of boules.

All in all, I would say that the soirees and all that they entail have become the highlight of each month for me. We all really appreciate the set-up and have gradually become a wonderful sisterhood, which continues beyond the meetings to going to the theatre, concerts, walks etc.

A couple I know, Pat and John, have a Maori friend, Peter. They are all retired head teachers who enjoy walking together. Pat asked me if I would like to join them on any of their walks. I said I would, but I wanted to make it quite clear that I was not up for any matchmaking. This was readily understood because this gentleman is a widower of five years and like me, doesn't want any other commitments. We haven't actually been on a walk yet, but a few days later she rang to ask me if I would make up a foursome to go out for dinner and since everything seemed to be perfectly understood, I could see no reason not to go! He was a very nice gentleman, full of fun, and we all had a very pleasant evening.

21

I have just experienced the most glorious Easter! The weather was hot and sunny – but the thing that really brought great cheer to me was the wonderful group of friends that I shared it with.

Jan and Andrew are away doing one of those week-long walks in the bush. The sort of activity the young, or utterly mad, seem to relish. So I was resigned to be spending the holiday alone. I am gradually becoming a 'big girl' now and am accepting the fact that I have to fend for myself, but my phone was ringing constantly and I spent the whole holiday socialising. I was hardly at home at all. As a fairly recent newcomer, I felt very privileged to be included in all the activities of the new friends I have made. By the end of the holiday, I was glad to collapse into bed and have a good rest!

'I wake each morning with the thrill of expectation and the joy of being truly alive. And I'm thankful for this day.' (Angela L Wozniak.)

Regardless of all this, I still miss Colin so very much, but at least the waterfall seems to have abated.

My dear little cat continues to surprise and delight me. He follows me everywhere, which I suppose is only natural since he knew nothing of the outside world until he was about six months old. We go about our lives in harmony and I must confess to actually talking to him. If anybody could here me talking to both Colin and the cat, I'm sure I would be hastily committed.

I really love our old suite of furniture, but it is rather uncomfortable, so I have recently bought myself a new reclining chair. It's absolutely delightful, so comfortable. I really love it, but so does someone else! He looks so cosy that I hate to move him and find myself collapsing back into one of the old chairs!

The Governor General recently visited Christchurch and a grand black tie dinner was planned for him. I went along to that with some friends – I thought I ought – the Governor General would never have forgiven me if I hadn't! At least it gave me chance to resurrect one of my evening gowns, so that made me happy. I still miss the old days when I was entertaining, with all the glamour, the dressing-up and adoration involved. I simply loved to transform myself from an ordinary little granny into an elegant *grande dame*.

'My only regret in the theatre is that I could never sit out front and watch me.' (John Barrymore.)

'Oh that we had some power to see ourselves as others see us!' (Robert Burns.)

Everyone has been so kind about my undernourished state. New and old friends have shown so much concern, it's all been so comforting to me. My own dear daughter Jan has given me her input. When I told her about it all and how everyone was being so incredibly kind to me, her comment was that I needed a 'good kick up the arse' and I should 'get myself in gear'. Ah well, I suppose you have to face reality and can rely on your loved ones to help you!

I continue to go to all that Christchurch offers intellectually and have recently been to a wonderful Tchaikovsky recital in the cathedral. I have even been invited to join a group of friends for a walk around one of the surrounding mountains. I really thought I ought to go, but to tell the truth I certainly wasn't relishing it. I'm just not the outdoor type. In the end, I had to hurriedly shorten a pair of trousers in order to don a pair of sensible flat walking shoes and loaded my backpack in preparation for the great trip outdoors! I'll spare you all the gory details, but if I say that the whole walk lasted four hours, you will understand that I was practically crawling the last three and a half! I really felt like one of those actors dragging themselves across the dusty, arid desert, gasping for a drink – I'm not talking about alcohol here, just plain, good, clear water.

During the trip I discovered that I have a heart that thumps rather loudly, I have a pair of thighs that scream out with pain, I have a pair of feet that feel as though they are made of lead, I have underdeveloped lungs that gasp for breath and that I actually like . . . water! Yes water! I couldn't get enough of it. In spite of all this, the outstanding views all around certainly sweetened the burden of it all. It was absolutely magnificent.

When I eventually arrived home and checked it out on the map, I just couldn't believe that I had covered so much ground. They say exercise is good for you but I must confess, I didn't feel it at the time. Even after a good night's sleep, I was still wilting! Let's just say that I don't think I will be rushing out to buy a pair of walking boots.

The last month has been incredibly busy for me. I flew up to Wellington to visit the family – they all seem to be jogging along very happily and quite settled in their new lives now. Sue and I spent our days wining, dining and shopping! So no complaints there!

On my return to Christchurch, I had hardly landed before my social life was in full swing again. I even had two calls on my mobile as I was driving home from the airport.

One hot sunny day, Jan decided that she wanted her horse, York, to have a paddle in the ocean. She brought him in his truck to my house where he alighted and steadfastly clip-clopped down to the beach. They both walked along the beach in the sea as I followed on the promenade, stopping occasionally to take photographs.

People who walk their dogs usually carry a plastic bag in which to collect their droppings and it rather amused me to see Jan gather together several old shopping carriers for the same purpose. It didn't seem quite so amusing when I realised that it would actually be me having to shovel up huge piles of you know what – which rather cramped my style!

After walking back to the house, we sat on the back patio having a lovely lunch in the sunshine together with the customary glass of cool wine. All the while, York was roaming around the garden, feasting on the lawn, while continuing to make piles of droppings everywhere! I thought how much he seemed to remind me of a factory, with material going in one end, being immediately processed in preparation for delivery the other! The garden is quite sizable, so he was able to graze happily – under supervision. It did seem rather odd to see a huge horse wandering around a suburban garden!

This month was rather special in that it was Wesley's eighteenth birthday and I felt rather honoured that he chose to come to Christchurch, and spend it with me. That caused me to think hard about a suitable birthday treat for an eighteen-year-old. I decided to take him and his girlfriend, together with Jan and Andrew, out for a special meal. But would that be exciting enough, I wondered? Then I had an idea that absolutely delighted him.

As we are all too aware, someone has to drive and not drink on these occasions, so I decided that no-one would have to feel deprived of anything and booked to have a chauffeur-driven stretch limo pick us up. The car arrived all shiny and white and the chauffeur stood to attention as we all got in with great glee!

Inside was a well-equipped bar with glasses and champagne, and windows bordered with disco lights which pulsated with the music. The sort of thing that fills me with horror but nevertheless, I conceded that it did seem to make the ride more jolly!

'If one hears bad music it is one's duty to drown it in conversation.' (Oscar Wilde.)

As it happened, Wes and his girlfriend sat in awe of it all, while his auntie and granny got totally into the experience and started bopping around and 'hand jiving'.

It really was great fun and nice to know that we would be picked up at the end of the evening, too. I asked the driver if he would give us an extra treat by driving home along the summit road, skimming the very tops of the mountains, which have the most awe-inspiring views of the city, even more exciting when illuminated. All in all, I feel we had a very memorable evening.

Wes had told me that he is saving for a sports car; I thought this was quite appropriate:

> One day a chicken was walking through a meadow when she saw a horse stuck in the mud. Thinking fast, she got the farmer's sports car, tied one end of a rope to the bumper and the other to the horse and pulled the horse to safety. The following week the horse was walking through the meadow and saw the chicken stuck in the mud. Thinking fast, he told the chicken to hold on to his willy while he pulled her to safety. And the moral of this story is if you're hung like a horse you don't need a flash sports car to pick up chicks.

I wonder if he will take note of this advice from his sweet little old granny!

A few days later I was busy preparing for a visit down to Queenstown to my old theatrical friends. Although I have been living here three years now, I must say that I never cease to marvel at the wonderful sights of nature here in NZ. The flight from Christchurch to Queenstown passes over the Southern Alps and although the sun was shining, there had been a heavy snowfall that topped the mountains with a cosy white blanket.

Alfred and Barbara had recently moved into a newly built bungalow. The move had disturbed the layout of the wardrobe that I had helped Barbara with on a previous visit, so out came everything again and I had a wonderful time doing what I love best, sorting and reorganising. As ever, she was delighted to have everything 'colour coded' and placed in various sections for the seasons. It gave me great pleasure too as after years organising classrooms, I just have to have everything labelled and in place, even in the house. After a very relaxing and cosy week of wining, dining and reminiscing, I began to think that old friends are like old shoes – so comfortable and good to slip into!

As we are all ageing, it also made me wonder if we had ever actually done the things we talked about or had it just been a dream. Oh – how our lives (and bodies!) have changed.

'Of all the things that wisdom provides to help one live one's entire life in happiness – the greatest by far is the possession of friendship.' (Epicurus.)

'I have everything I had twenty years ago, only it's all a little bit lower.' (Gypsy Rose Lee.)

Who ever said that times flies by as you get older was certainly right!

My Sumner Soiree, first group, continues to flourish and I now have another group, which started this year in January, so that keeps me busy twice a month. It works so well because it gives me a chance to do all that I enjoy and the ladies seem to love it too. Since they are what I call 'privileged', meaning never having to work, they arrive with plates of wonderful cuisine to share.

Left to me it would be 'If in doubt, add more wine.' (Curnonsky.)

Now for some rather amazing news. I am to resurrect my 'Last Night of the Proms' act – and this is how it all came about. I was recently introduced to a retired farmer and his wife and they proved to be a rather interesting couple. Theirs is no longer a working farm and the farmer is now devoting his time to collecting and restoring old farm equipment. He was telling me that, since it involves searching the country for several examples of the same model, it could take up to three years just to restore one old tractor. When he has enough material, he takes pieces from each to create something that is eventually restored and in running order again. Consequently, he has many barns full of really old farming equipment. Not a pretty sight – it reminded me of Steptoe's yard, nevertheless very satisfying for him. There are meetings all over NZ of these old relics so he is kept very happily occupied.

His wife, Bev, was very keen on pursuing a hobby in music and was having weekly organ lessons. She wanted to demonstrate her skills and we all enjoyed a little concert by her. Actually, she was playing a lot of the stuff I used to sing, so after a while, I started to tentatively sing along. The first time for four years, I might add.

A few days later, I received a phone call from someone whose voice I didn't recognise, which was rather embarrassing because it turned out to be Bev. She asked me if I would sing to her accompaniment for a function on the following Sunday. I can't say that I relished the idea, but she was so nice and full of enthusiasm that I felt I ought to give it a go, so off I went, having no idea of what she actually wanted me to sing! The hall was huge and it was full of organ enthusiasts who took it in turns to entertain each other. When it was Bev's turn, she played a couple of pieces and then introduced me. I was so incredibly nervous that I felt sure they would see my heart thumping away and hear the slight shake in my voice. Anyway, they thought I was the best thing since sliced bread, and I am booked to do my 'Last Night of the Proms' act on 24th April – Anzac Day, the equivalent of our Remembrance Day!

I came home slightly shell shocked at my performance after so many years of silence, but they all seemed to enjoy it so very much. Could it be that they were very elderly and not only hard of hearing, but with faltering sight too? I feel I ought to 'Spread a Little Happiness' (one of the songs I used to sing and one of Colin's favourites) so off I go again!

One of my Christchurch friends moved into an enormous house on the banks of the River Avon. It was originally a very beautiful house and she had many alterations, which took about a year to complete. When all was done, she had a house warming garden party to which I was invited.

The invitation said it was to be a *White Mischief* theme. If you are not familiar with the story, it was set in Kenya and was all about the privileged classes of the early 1940s. People were coming in all sorts of outfits, even some in African gear. Of course, I chose to dress as a 'Titled Lady', dripping with pearls and diamonds (false, of course!).

A huge marquee was erected on the lawns, which swept down to the river where she had a landing stage of her very own. Caterers supplied a wonderful dinner and suitable background music was being played, so what with the wonderful weather, you can imagine how stylish the whole occasion was – just my cup of tea.

22

We have celebrated my dear Sir Edward Elgar's first birthday. It was during a week when one of my Sumner Soirees was due to take place, so I decided to have a birthday party and invite all his aunties (the Soiree ladies).

Donning myself all in black with a leopard-skin belt, scarf, tights and shoes, plus a pair of leopard ears on a headband – because my darling looks just like a baby leopard – my ladies squealed with surprise and delight when I opened the door to them.

They had brought their usual selection of goodies for us all to enjoy for lunch and I supplied some bubbles for a toast to Sir Edward, plus a birthday cake that I had had made especially for the occasion.

Before the ladies arrived, after I had set everything out, I had found the birthday boy himself sitting on the table eating his cake! I hurriedly scooped away the remains from the place where he had been eating, with the intention of throwing the bits and pieces in the bin and covering the hole with the 'Happy Birthday' label. As it was, after years of automatically eating all the leftovers from my little girls' meals, I completely forgot it was 'the cat' and before I knew what had happened, I had put the whole lot in my mouth. This then caused me to have a completely sleepless night sweating and worrying because I thought I could feel foot and mouth disease coming on.

Back to the story. As usual everyone enjoyed the lunch, and we all raised our glasses to Sir Edward and consumed the remains of the cake. Then our attention was drawn to a little present that had been placed on the table for Sir Edward. It was so sweet. The label said: 'For Elgar Sweetie, with cuddles and loads of love from Mummy, Auntie Jan (who rescued you) and all your other aunties (assembled here and far away in England).' As I opened it, there appeared a beautiful black velvet neckband, studied with diamante. With a little encouragement from me, we all agreed that he deserved no less and merrily sang 'Happy Birthday', raising yet another glass of bubbles!

I then set a quiz for the ladies (forever the teacher!) to see who could think of the most words beginning with 'cat'. They all seemed to enjoy that little exercise and the winner went away with a tiny glass cat that I had found in the $2 shop. The entertainment that followed was a DVD of Andrew Lloyd Webber's *Cats* (based on *Old Possum's Book of Practical Cats* by T.S. Eliot). I am pleased to say that the birthday party was thoroughly enjoyed by everyone, although the whole event had proved to be too exciting for the little darling himself since he had chosen to sneak through his cat-flap and go for a stroll in the garden. To complete the celebrations, I had made a souvenir commemorative programme for each lady to take away. I had been lucky enough to find a greetings card picturing a little cat, standing upright with baton in hand conducting an orchestra, which seemed most appropriate. Each had a card containing all the different 'cat' acts of the show.

Everyone agreed how much they had enjoyed the occasion, so I felt very happy about all the effort I had put in to make it so special for Sir Edward. He has taken to his new collar and struts around the garden showing off the sparkling diamantes.

I've had a treat myself this month. I went with a group of the Christchurch ladies for a short break to a reciprocal club in Melbourne. Much to my surprise, Melbourne is incredibly large, full of grand buildings plus the usual skyscrapers – a real city of style and art. I'm sorry to say that, in comparison, dear old London looked like a little provincial city!

We stayed at a ladies' club, formed in around 1840. A most interesting feature was a long corridor lined with photographs of all the lady presidents from the very beginning. As one looked along the walls, it was incredible to observe the gradual change in the ladies over the years, from the Victorian era to the present day.

The changes were not only in dress, but also hairstyles and the manner in which they were sitting. As time progressed, the faces and expressions of the ladies began to change too and by the time the photographs reached the last decade, one could see an amazing difference in their attitude; the confident stance and the way in which they were looking directly into the camera. It was a graphic illustration of the progress of society since the Victorian era and one that I found completely fascinating.

One of the past presidents was Dame Elizabeth Murdock and we were invited to visit her in her country retreat. Everyone in Melbourne speaks highly of her and says what a sweet, kind and generous lady she is, so I was really looking forward to meeting her. As you might imagine, the mansion itself was set in sweeping grounds, and the gracious lady was grandly seated ready to welcome us all. At ninety-nine years old, she had the body of a little old lady but she was as bright as any of us younger people there and spoke briskly and without hesitation. Not at all as you might expect a lady of that age to converse. She had a beautiful face and you could see the kindness therein.

Somebody asked if they could take a photograph of her and she readily agreed. Having witnessed that, I asked if I might have a photograph taken with her and, again, she graciously agreed. As I bobbed down beside her chair, I whispered in her ear that I had come all the way from England and felt very privileged to have a photograph taken with what I considered to be Australian royalty. Her reply was to laugh, saucily slap my hand and say, 'Oh – you silly little girl!' She really was a little sweetie.

Another outing was to a production of *My Fair Lady*, and what a stunning occasion that was. The concert hall, like everything else in Melbourne, was enormous and very grandly decorated and the production itself was spectacular. Set design so cleverly executed, costumes stunning, actors first class, music, as ever, delightful but the only disappointing thing was that it was in a foreign language ... Australian! Honestly, it all seemed so incongruous and I just couldn't identify with anything that sounded English and especially Cockney! What a shame. They just didn't manage to capture the accent.

Back home in Christchurch, the very next night, I went to a production of Alan Bennett's *The History Boys,* a play set in a boy's school trying hard to get its pupils into Oxford. Funny and heartfelt arguments on the purpose of education are explored between the pupils and staff in this witty and clever play. Alan Bennett, being a grounded Yorkshireman, had obviously spotted the pretension and falsity of the snobbery therein and made a thought-provoking comedy out of it all. So clever of him!

As ever, Christchurch had put on an excellent production worthy of any West End stage. How lucky I feel to have it all on my doorstep!

I've had the usual round of dinners and lunches to attend, all of which have been very pleasant, but the novelty of all that is wearing a little thin now and I feel just as happy to stay indoors stroking Sir Edward!

The month seems mainly to have been taken up with yet another visit from Alfred and Barbara. The first thing they like to do is 'hit the shops'. Since they live in a rather remote area with very limited shopping, they are pleased to sample the delights of a major city's wares. They always seem to go home with something special.

We had several memorable meals out and even a mid-winter dinner here, to which I invited Jan and Andrew, plus his mother and father. After a few of my silly games etc. it proved to be a jolly occasion.

Lyttelton had a mid-winter Festival of Lights, so we went along to that. The main street was closed and lined with stalls laden with all sorts of goodies. They had a parade, which was ablaze with candles. There were many activities, including a masked ball, but being ever mindful of our age, I chose to book a restaurant right on the harbour which overlooked the boats with their lights aglow.

Another evening we went to The Red Rose Dinner Theatre, where a group of people put on a production while the audience dines. It was based on the English music hall, so that was especially interesting to us. The content of the show was good. Music, costumes etc. excellent, but it just didn't seem to 'gel' and certainly lacked lustre. Could it be the accent again? It just didn't come across so well. It lacked the spontaneity, warmth and general excitement of a real London music hall.

In Christchurch we have two trains that are especially for tourists. The Coastal Pacific runs along the coast to Picton at the top of the South Island, and the other, the TranzAlpine, runs across from Christchurch to Greymouth on the West Coast. Since it is winter, I booked for a trip on the TranzAlpine and we weren't disappointed. The snowfall certainly proved to be an exceedingly pretty sight, covering the lush terrain and magnificent trees. I was sitting next to an Australian gentleman who had never experienced snow firsthand before, and he was really excited, taking numerous photographs to capture this new experience. The train stopped for a while to allow folk to get off and spend a little time in the snow and when he arrived back inside, he was amazed at how frozen he felt. With the journey taking four hours each way, we were quite weary by the time we reached home and were glad to tumble into our warm beds early that night.

The very best entertainment I have left to last! It was a Berlin Burlesque, an incredible evening featuring music hall, Vaudeville and cabaret music, with lush, colourful costumes, dramatic lighting, pastiche, parody and wit. The Berlin Burlesque mixed it all up with the finest dancing girls, chanson singers, exotic pole dancers showing all their wares and more, breaking all the rules while featuring the most famous of all the cabaret singers, Marlene Dietrich (not the real one!). One of the acts, judging by the uproar, shocked the socks off me and everyone else. It was a very handsome young man with a most beautiful body who did an acrobatic act, showing off his glorious body to perfection (dribble, dribble!). But – wait for it – ending his act featuring his . . . I'm getting overcome as I write! . . . his naked penis! The whole hall was electric! Both women and men were stamping their feet, banging their tables, screaming, whistling and clapping with delight, especially my daughter Jan. I thought she'd have a seizure, she screamed so much!

Who would have thought that dear little pure New Zealand, the very end of the world, would have had such a thing? It must have been as good as anything in Vegas. It proved to be one of the most exciting evenings ever.

We have just had the most horrendous thunderstorm I have ever experienced. The first bang really sounded as though someone was bashing the door, trying to get in. Both Elgar and I woke with a start and sat up feeling very alarmed (we sleep together now!).

That was quickly followed by further crashes and then I realised it was actually a thunderstorm. Since I sleep with the blinds open, the whole room was being lit just like those horrid flashing lights the young have at their discos. What with the clapping of the thunder, the howling of the wind and the flashing of lights, it seemed as though we were in the middle of a Dracula movie or might expect to be visited by the Hound of the Baskervilles. My only comfort was Sir Edward!

Once the thunder had abated, the hail stones started, only, once again, like nothing I have heard before. In NZ the houses mainly have tin roofs so they do tend to magnify the sound, but these particular hail stones really sounded like great house bricks being hurled down. All in all, it was an astounding experience and something I don't relish happening again. God sure was in a bad temper that night!

'The way I see it, if you want the rainbow you gotta put up with the rain.' (Dolly Parton.)

In spite of the severe weather, there are wonderful signs of spring. The trees are in blossom, and the gracious weeping willows that edge the River Avon are developing new green shoots. I have seen the pair of black swans with their little family and that in itself is a heartening sight. They say that swans are faithful to each other, which is a beautiful notion, but I felt that I was actually witnessing the love they have for each other. The loving parents were attentively watching their little family, darting to and fro, exploring and pecking whilst they were keeping guard.

23

Horror of horrors! Emergency alert! Having been away for a while, I returned to find that the big double garage at the back of the property had been infested with rats! Just like a snowfall, it was covered with black rat droppings. It was absolutely astounding. You could never have believed such a sight. Rat droppings were absolutely everywhere. On the floor, across the shelves, in boxes, absolutely everywhere!

Fortunately, one of my grandsons was visiting me, so between the two of us we started to tackle the problem. The floor was so thick that we couldn't even walk in until Wes had hoovered a path for us.

Then started the job of removing everything out of the garage onto the courtyard. We started at 8.30 a.m. and worked continuously, eventually coming in at 2.30 p.m. We both stripped out of our clothes, which immediately went into the washing machine and we had baths and showers. The stuff they had ruined totalled eight large boxes and bags which were far too much for the usual dust-cart and had to be taken to the tip in a van. Since the rats had been in every box and container that was on the shelves, I lost no end of really good stuff, including a brand new garden pagoda that was torn to shreds by their teeth. I was absolutely devastated.

On a more cheery note. I continue to find new things to do and manage to keep myself happily busy. Just recently I have discovered a group called Operatunity. Although they are now 'past their sell-by date', they are wonderfully trained singers who have performed all over the world and now travel around NZ giving monthly concerts in each district. The shows they give usually last for around two hours and each concert has a different theme. For example 'Puccini, Verdi and Mozart – Stage and Screen' included all the favourite songs from those wonderful Hollywood musicals; 'The Americans' featured Kern, Gershwin and Berlin, and many more from a wide spectrum of wonderful music. A local cinema also puts on monthly films about the great composers, their life history and work. The last film I saw was about Beethoven was all very interesting but rather long – three hours!

Do you realise that Colin has been deceased five years now? I still miss him so much.

I have just had my sixty-eighth birthday! As they say, the years certainly fly by, especially as you get older.

'No woman should ever be quite accurate about her age. It looks so calculating.' (Oscar Wilde.)

I now have new next-door neighbours. They were planning a family skiing trip – he has a family of four boys! I ask myself if, after four boys, they might have realised what was causing it! Since he didn't want to lose work while away, he asked me if I would man the phone for the week and keep his appointments in order. Being a doctor's wife, with experience of that kind, it seemed a good thing to do and I actually enjoyed being out there in the work force again.

I continue to attend Jan's horse events and entertain her fellow equestrians in the back of the horse truck with fresh salmon and bubbles etc. Needless to say, I seem to be very popular!

Entertainment of all kinds continues to flourish in Christchurch and they have recently had a winter festival with a huge ice rink erected in Cathedral Square. The 'Ice Dome' catered for skaters of all ages and abilities to slip, slide, or pirouette their way around the rink. Obviously, I didn't partake but it was highly amusing to watch those who did.

I've just returned from a holiday in Cairns, Australia. It seemed a good idea at the time of booking, but, I now find that I have settled so well in my new life that, although it was a pleasant interlude, I felt very pleased to return home to my lovely house and garden and was reminded of something Colin used to say – that he'd rather enjoy his own back yard. After a lifetime of work etc. I'm inclined to agree with him and I find that it is a very satisfying feeling.

On returning home and picking up Sir Edward Elgar from the cattery, I was sorry to find that he had caught some sort of cat flu. Another visit to the vets. I am now realising that vets must earn as much as doctors! After an injection and a course of antibiotics and being faced with a hefty bill, I remarked to the vet that this little vagrant from the mountains seemed to be financing his summer holidays! He actually laughed (all the way to the bank, no doubt!) which was quite refreshing since the NZ folk don't seem to understand my British humour.

Unfortunately the treatment prescribed didn't clear up Elgar's health problems and he has been really poorly since mid-July. His regular vet just couldn't seem to get to the bottom of it all, although he had kept him at the surgery for four days of observation, so I felt obliged to take him to a veterinary hospital for a second opinion. They also kept him for a couple of days. Think cash tills frantically registering here! He had endless tests and I was eventually able to bring him home, but had to take him back each day for his medication. That in itself proved to be quite stressful since, like most animals, he just doesn't like going in his carry cage. When I originally went to collect him and bring him home the vet asked me if I had anyone to help with the medication and of course I have Jan, so that was deemed to be all right. At that point I had no idea of the relevance of the vet's question. Sir Edward had to have a tablet twice a day and a syringe of white liquid each morning, so now I will tell you why I have to take him back to the surgery each day.

First attempt at giving Sir Edward his medication – Elgar on my lap with me firmly holding his front paws – Jan approaches with the syringe, forces his mouth open and squirts – Elgar moves his head, she misses and I am covered with the white runny mixture (I might mention here that I had an appointment in town that day and was dressed accordingly!). Second attempt – Elgar still in my iron grip – Jan manages to get the stuff into his mouth – Elgar turns and spits it back out all over me again! Third attempt – Elgar has now disappeared upstairs, hiding under my bed. Jan moans like hell at me for having left the door open. We both go up, me one side of the bed with a bowl of food in order to entice him out and Jan the other, with a broom handle in case he needs just that little more encouragement! All this happened at approximately 8 a.m. and Elgar didn't surface until 12 noon! That is why I have to take him in every day for his medication.

How To Give A Cat A Pill:

1. Pick up cat and cradle it in the crook of your left arm as if holding a baby. Position right forefinger and thumb on either side of cat's mouth and gently apply pressure to cheeks while holding pill in right hand. As cat opens mouth, pop pill into mouth. Allow cat to close mouth and swallow.
2. Retrieve pill from floor and cat from behind sofa. Cradle cat in left arm and repeat process.
3. Retrieve cat from bedroom, and throw soggy pill away.
4. Take new pill from foil wrap, cradle cat in left arm, holding rear paws tightly with left hand. Force jaws open and push pill to back of mouth with right forefinger. Hold mouth shut for a count of ten.
5. Retrieve pill from goldfish bowl and cat from top of wardrobe. Call spouse from garden.
6. Kneel on floor with cat wedged firmly between knees, hold front and rear paws. Ignore low growls emitted by cat. Get spouse to hold head firmly with one hand while forcing wooden ruler into mouth. Drop pill down ruler and rub cat's throat vigorously.
7. Retrieve cat from curtain rail, get another pill from foil wrap.

Make note to buy new ruler and repair curtains. Carefully sweep shattered figurines and vases from hearth and set to one side for gluing later.

8. Wrap cat in large towel and get spouse to lie on cat with head just visible from below armpit. Put pill in end of drinking straw, force mouth open with pencil and blow down drinking straw.

9. Check label to make sure pill not harmful to humans, drink one beer to take taste away. Apply Band-Aid to spouse's forearm and remove blood from carpet with cold water and soap.

10. Retrieve cat from neighbour's shed. Get another pill. Open another beer. Place cat in cupboard, and close door onto neck, to leave head showing. Force mouth open with dessert spoon. Flick pill down throat with elastic band.

11. Fetch screwdriver from garage and put cupboard door back on hinges. Drink beer. Fetch bottle of Scotch. Pour shot, drink. Apply cold compress to cheek and check records for date of last tetanus shot. Apply whisky compress to cheek to disinfect. Toss back another shot. Throw T-shirt away and fetch new one from bedroom.

12. Call fire department to retrieve the damn cat from across the road. Apologise to neighbour who crashed into fence while swerving to avoid cat. Take last pill from foil wrap.

13. Tie the little bastard's front paws to rear paws with garden twine and bind tightly to leg of dining table, find heavy-duty pruning gloves from shed. Push pill into mouth followed by large piece of fillet steak. Be rough about it. Hold head vertically and pour two pints of water down throat to wash pill down.

14. Consume remainder of Scotch. Get spouse to drive you to the emergency room, sit quietly while doctor stitches fingers and forearm and removes pill remnants from right eye. Call furniture shop on way home to order new table.

15. Arrange for RSPCA to collect mutant cat from hell and call local pet shop to see if they have any hamsters.

How To Give A Dog A Pill:

1. Wrap it in bacon.
2. Toss it in the air.
   (Unknown.)

The very last test that the vet thought might throw some light on the problem was to have an operation which involved a camera inserted into his back passage. I made light of things by asking if it was to be one of those old Box Brownies, which as its name suggests is a large brown box. I had spent a fortune on this dear little man from the mountains and arrived at the conclusion that if he were still living in the wilderness nature would determine if he survived or not, so I opted to save him the indignities of the camera.

Frankly, I don't feel too much of a failure since the vet has told me that he is an exceptionally big cat and is very determined. I have often watched him in the garden and thought how big he is and how much he resembles a tiger which, bearing in mind he is a feral cat, is hardly surprising. I won't tell you how much all this has cost me except to say the bill, so far, has run into four figures! Never mind – I love him and that's that.

My Sumner Soiree continues to flourish, so much so that I am often asked by the ladies if they may bring a friend along. Unfortunately, I felt it was not possible to expand the group for two reasons. Since the group already consists of ten ladies, the house couldn't comfortably accommodate more. Also it could upset the balance of the 'sisterhood' that has developed. The next suggestion was that I should hire a hall and do a presentation once a month on a grander scale. There were also two reasons not to pursue that idea. The obvious one is that all the DVDs in my collection clearly state that they are not for 'public' viewing, and I certainly would not want to break any laws. The other was that I felt the whole thing was becoming too big a commitment for me – it would be like working again.

A LEAP INTO THE UNKNOWN

I have now formed a second group, which also meets in my home, so as you can imagine the two groups keep me busy.

My other piece of news is far more interesting. I have turned into Lady Chatterley! After four years of working hard in the garden and finding that, due to my ignorance, everything I plant promptly dies, I decided to bring in a professional and have the garden completely redesigned and planted. Enter one gorgeous, young, good looking, charming, talented, delightful, sensitive – gay– landscape gardener. He is everything I like!

He has completely transformed the garden – he's found wonderful positions for all my statues and special features and has even designed and built a special pagoda for Colin's memorial seat. With his wonderful flare, he has also arranged each feature to be illuminated in the evenings for my delight. I now sit looking at my very own piece of heaven on earth and for the first time in my life, I marvel at the contentment I have at last found.

This beautiful young man seems to have really taken a shine to me and it is not unusual for him to ring and say, 'Hello Gorgeous,' he isn't blind or deaf, I hasten to add, 'I'm in your area, I'll call in for a glass of wine.' And me trying to give it up – the wine I mean.

He arrives and settles in for an evening of exchanging experiences. I realise the attraction I hold for him. I am a mature lady with a past in entertainment and with albums full of sumptuous costumes to drool over and stories of exciting escapades. Even I find me interesting!

He even loves Sir Edward Elgar as I do! What more could I want? We really get on so well and enjoy each other's company. He is wonderfully appreciative and I am a very happy bunny. Being a 'has been', I now have a charming companion who seems to really admire me. I don't doubt for one minute that he will move on to more exciting projects, but for the time being I am really enjoying his company.

Important announcement; I wish to state that my love affair with Sir Edward Elgar is over. I have recently witnessed him lie flat on his tummy and crawl under the decking outside the house, and emerge with the dearest little fat mouse in his mouth. After my banging and rattling the French doors, he dropped the aforesaid and commenced playing with the poor mouse by chasing it, tapping it, picking it up, throwing it down and generally tantalising it.

After more shouting and banging from me, he carried the little soul off into the undergrowth. Realising that in the face of nature, I could do no more, I settled down for some intellectual stimulation in the form of one of my CDs. Trying to block the horrors from my mind, I began to relax and slipped into a delightful reverie when the monster sauntered in with the mangled remains of the mouse dangling from his mouth! Knowledgeable friends have since informed me that he was only trying to please me with his proud achievement.

I am always being accused of over-feeding him and he has had nothing but expensive 'health' food from the vets since his illness. In conclusion, I think that he is one fat greedy bastard who, in spite of all my loving care, has been going out for 'takeaways'.

I now wish to state that I like neither titled gentlemen nor cats. Two days later, after not speaking to him of the horror and giving him the 'cold shoulder' and 'evil eye' treatment, I am beginning to recover from it all and, dare I admit, I continue to allow him to snuggle up and sleep on my bed with me! Oh dear – how fickle can one get?

Just recently, my two eldest grandsons decided to come to Christchurch for a mini holiday with me. Naturally, I was delighted and took them around and about. I haven't laughed so much for ages. It was great fun.

We spent many interesting evenings sitting on the deck, drink in hand, deep in conversation – and I'm pleased to inform you that they opened their hearts and told me all their secrets – uncensored!

We had been to the supermarket and the drink they favoured was something called Viva a Sol. It was such a nice refreshing beer that when we were eating out in a rather stylish restaurant one evening, I said to the waiter that I would like a Viva a Sol. The boys burst into laughter and I really didn't understand why. They pointed out that the beer was actually called Sol and they had added the rest. This meant that a sweet little old granny like me had actually said to the waiter Viva Arse Ole. Oh dear, oh dear, and there I was smugly thinking I was up there with the young crowd requesting a nice refreshing lightweight beer rather than my usual wine. Ah well, at least it gave them a laugh and I felt quite pleased to be told I 'crack them up' (their expression).

Before they returned home I was able to give them each a very special gift. Ever since I had my own little girls and then my grandchildren, I have taken photographs of their development. For the past few months I have been filling photograph albums of their progress, dating each and every photograph. It has been a very interesting and moving task for me. With all complete, I have been making grand presentations of them to the individuals and I must say that I am delighted with their reception. They all, unanimously, found them a revelation and assured me they would treasure them always. How very satisfying for me, since in the end all we have is love and memories. Since the advent of computers, many photographs stored that way have actually been lost, proving that the old ways are sometimes the safest.

After Jan continually saying I should take more exercise, I decided to actually go for a 'health giving' walk last Sunday. There are two routes to the village, one along the seafront promenade and the other along the road. Since I have usually chosen to take visitors along the promenade, I decided to take the more direct route along the road. Being Sunday, the shops don't open until late morning so I decided to aim to reach the village in the region of elevenish and perhaps stop for a leisurely coffee. It was an absolutely beautiful morning and I was enjoying ambling along in the sun. Something seemed rather strange, since I met no other person out and about. When I reached the village, it seemed even stranger because there was absolutely no-one about and the shops were all closed. This must be some sort of public holiday, I thought, but even that idea seemed odd since Sumner, being a seaside resort, is usually buzzing with activity whatever the season. Anyway, after feeling as though

I had walked into a gunfight at Deadwood City, I thought the only thing was to saunter back home.

I spent the rest of the day happily lazing in the garden, doing odds and ends and eventually came in for the six o'clock news. I got one almighty shock! Apparently there had been a devastating earthquake in Chile, which was affecting New Zealand and our very own coast was on major alert. Earlier in the day, everyone had been advised to be prepared to vacate their homes for higher ground and safety! Helicopters were flying up and down the coast and everyone was heeding the warning and heading for safety. Everyone but me!

All the locals had gone into panic mode and had driven with laden cars up to the very top of the mountain. They were watching the tide chase in and out and at the same time having a wonderfully social day wining and dining from the comfort and safety of their vantage point. When I moved from England I decided not to watch the news anymore. All my life I have watched the news, become terribly worried and felt totally helpless as to what difference I could make to anything, so when I moved I decided I would just let the world spin around me and try to relax in my ignorance. That proved to be a mistake.

It was so serious that even all the big container ships and liners were taken out of Lyttelton Harbour. Although so far away, the shock of Chile was causing extremely fast movement in the ocean around us and the waves were rushing in much faster than usual.

Because of this incident, many friends have registered me on their 'warning list'. I ought to tell some of them not to bother otherwise they might be trapped trying to get through to me when, this time, it could be me who is safely at the top of the mountain, imbibing!

Ah well – you can't say life is boring here, can you?

23

Since arriving in NZ nearly five years ago, I have written approximately sixty emails and letters home to everyone, full of the trials and tribulations of relocating, at an advanced age, to the other side of the world.

I am at last becoming so adjusted to my new life that I hardly think anything is different and interesting enough to report home about anymore.

I have now settled down into a comfortable social life consisting of the usual lunch dates, dinner parties, theatre, concerts, bridge, Mahjong, walks, etc. with the occasional outdoor sports activities thrown in (unheard of for the English me).

My dearly loved home in England, which I so reluctantly left, is becoming a sad and sorry memory. I must confess to liking the house that I own now much better – it seems just perfect for my new lifestyle. My wardrobe has metamorphosised from the smart city wear of English towns to the more relaxed gear of the sports activities and country lifestyle of NZ. Even my trusted Burberry coats have now been joined by an anorak. In short, I seem to have a foot in each country and it really doesn't seem to be so very unusual anymore.

Although I have found the loss of my dear Colin to be the most painful experience I have ever known, I must confess to at last enjoying the freedom of doing whatever I please without any concern for another. For the first time ever, I have a little pet of my own and my dear Sir Edward Elgar seems to have brought this empty house alive. I didn't realise that one could love an animal so very much.

I have my two girls nearby and that is the best thing ever. I am so grateful for a second chance to show them how much I love them. I think that it is so sad that when we are young and trying to develop our own personalities and are so anxiously striving to keep everything ticking over in the home and workplace, we often neglect to spend quality time with the ones we love the most. My joy is that I have been given this second chance to centre all my attention on being a 'real' mum and granny – with no husband, no job and absolutely nothing to dilute my love for my offspring.

Together with the many emails and letters I have sent, I think I have just about given a good account of the journey I was forced to take five years ago on Colin's demise.

I have so much become a part of this country that I have now applied for NZ citizenship, have been accepted and yesterday attended the formal ceremony at the town hall, where I took the Oath of Allegiance and received a certificate and a native tree to plant in my garden.

I felt that it was the right thing to do, NZ being my adopted country, and this also means that I now have a NZ passport, which will be very handy when travelling on this side of the world. This will not affect my British status so I feel that I have done the right and proper thing and am officially part of both countries.

This is the Oath of Allegiance;

I (full name) swear that I will be faithful and bear true allegiance to Her Majesty Queen Elizabeth the Second, Queen of New Zealand, her heirs and successors according to law, and that I will faithfully observe the laws of New Zealand and fulfill my duties as a New Zealand citizen. So help me God.

I almost felt like adding after the 'Queen of NZ' bit 'and England'! I'll never let go of my inheritance and country of birth.

These are the words of the NZ national anthem, 'God Defend New Zealand':

God of nations at Thy feet,
In the bonds of love we meet,
Hear our voices, we entreat,
God defend our free land.
Guard Pacific's triple star,
From the shafts of strife and war,
Make her praises heard afar,
God defend New Zealand.

It really has been a memorable occasion for me because it is something I could never have dreamt of or planned, and yet it has been made so special for me by the wonderful response of all my new friends who have sent greetings cards, given me gifts (one being a NZ cookery book) and have even sung the NZ national anthem on my telephone answer machine!

25

I have written regularly for seven years now with stories about my new life. Just as I had decided that all was settled and stabilised, something has happened that is far more than I ever expected to have to cope with.

Earthquake: Saturday 4th September 2010, 4.30 a.m. – Report no. one:

Awoken in the middle of the night and obviously in bed, I had an experience that I never dreamt I would.

A bad earthquake is considered to have a magnitude in the region of 6 – this one was 7.4! It was truly frightening. Little did we know that an even more devastating earthquake was to come and that this time, people were not to be so lucky in escaping death.

In my bedroom, I have a dressing table with twelve drawers and each and every one of them flew out over the floor. Dear Elgar soon ran for cover under the bed. I was quite frightened about going downstairs, but knew I had to get out quickly so jumped out of bed – only to be thrown against the nearest wall. As it happened, the phone rang and when I eventually tracked it down somewhere on the floor, it was Jan to say she was coming round for me.

I had to tread over books and papers on my open landing where I have a sort of office and computer – the entire floor was covered.

Venturing downstairs, I found that the whole of the sitting room area and open-plan kitchen looking like a war zone, e.g. the cabinet that I store glasses in had flown open and glass was all over the floor. I simply can't list everything that occurred – it would take forever – but just to say quite honestly it was devastating.

As we were going to Jan's house, people were on the street considering it to be safer than indoors. The main quake seemed to have passed but then there were aftershocks and Andrew said even these were worse than any he had ever known.

We all had the radio on for reports and the civil defence people were on 'full crisis alert', issuing instructions on how we ought to be prepared to cope with anything further to come. For the first time in my life I didn't need laxatives to get me going! And that was not uncommon. Several of Jan's neighbours had gathered in her house and I can tell you that the loo was in good use that evening!

Reports came in that Christchurch central was instantly closed due to collapsed buildings, roads being ripped up, balconies collapsed, bridges broken, chimneys caving in on houses, shop fronts blown out, electricity failure and water mains flooding. Some buildings, we are told, are so badly damaged that they will have to be demolished! With the coming of dawn, we could see that all the flowerpots etc. in the garden were tipped over and Jan's ornamental pond was throwing water all over the place; the fish were flapping around on the grass, gasping for water.

Just across the road from Jan's there is a lovely green where the men play rugby in the winter and cricket in the summer. They won't be doing any of that for the time being because it is now all totally uneven and lumpy – we could see it moving just like the waves of an incoming tide!

The shocks and vibrations had actually reached all the way down the South Island and up to Wellington in the North Island, so that will confirm how violent it was. Andrew, who is in his forties, said that he has never known any quake like it before and assures me that it is unlikely to happen again for a very long time.

This is the message I sent in reply to English emails:

Thank you all so much for writing to me. It really was comforting to receive your emails.

Although the main quake seems to be over, we now have what they call aftershocks and these are pretty scary too. Since I had to hurry to dress when Jan collected me a 4.30 a.m. (middle of the night!) I decided to go to bed in my outdoor clothes last night – which was pretty uncomfortable but as it happened, I was glad that I did because there were about three more tremors.

It's an odd experience. You are lying in bed, all alone, trying to be brave and the bed starts to shake and slightly move, as in a shunting movement. I have a five-arm ornate chandelier just above my head and what with that swinging and rattling – you can imagine – I didn't get much sleep.

As for my titled gentleman, Sir Edward Elgar, he is permanently huddled under the bed, which actually is very sensible, since Civil Defence advise you to sit under a table. I really don't know what to do or where to go. I didn't fancy sitting under the dining room table all night but I suppose I should since I don't really relish being crowned by the crystals of the chandelier.

Oops – another tremor! And as I'm typing the computer is shaking! They say we can expect them for at least another two weeks! All this and yet I have had the most horrendous two weeks prior to the advent of the quake.

As you know, I lost a lot of my attributes to the cancer and have finally ended up with two dentures! With no teeth at the bottom, the denture sits quite nicely and doesn't bother me too much but although I had five teeth randomly left in the top of my mouth, it makes the top denture very hard to keep securely in place.

For quite some months now I have had a continual toothache in my bottom jaw, where there are no teeth! Well, one day I had the most horrendous pain and had to go to an emergency dentist. She told me I would need some extensive work done and would need to make a one and a half hour appointment – in the meantime she put a temporary filling in and while she was doing it, I was in absolute agony!

Despatched for home, I must confess to crying while trying to drive. I spent the whole night in the most dreadful pain ever and, by morning, I had to go to yet another emergency dentist. He X-rayed it and found it had been filled over an abscess! So – out it all came. To cut a long story short, I had to go back twice (both emergency appointments!) and after more extractions each time, have ended up with no teeth at all! My gum was sewn up and I have been told that I won't be able to be fitted for a new denture for at least a month, when they expect the swelling to have gone down! Poor me.

Added to all this, every time you need to go 'emergency' they tack an extra $50 on the bill – therefore with four emergency visits, the whole thing has cost well over $1000! No National Health in NZ!

All this, and I had to meet neighbours etc. during the quake crisis with my mouth caved in and my chin rising up to meet the tip of my nose, closely resembling Mr Punch! At least it gave them all a laugh and when I started fussing because, fleeing from the house so quickly, I hadn't had time to match my shoes and handbag with my outfit – they were in stitches!

Ah well, it's good to spread a little happiness occasionally. Next time we all meet, I am considering donning a paper bag over my head with eye-holes and long sexy lashes painted on. I could even draw some hair and a big smiley mouth with a full set of beautiful teeth. All joking apart, I am not relishing the coming weeks, what with all that the earthquake has brought, Christchurch closed down etc. – even a restaurant in the village caved in. It seems as though you really don't know where to go safely.

Hopefully, I will be able to keep you posted. In the meantime, please keep in touch – I find it so comforting.

Report no. two:
Well ... who'd a thought it! After all the traumas and changes of life since Colin passed away, this is something that I would never have imagined – being at the actual scene of a disaster. We are told on the news that is comparable with any major earthquake in the world where hundreds of thousands of people have died but ours was in the middle of the night when most people were at home in bed and not shopping in central Christchurch.

Even though I couldn't select my shoes, handbag and outfit for the day or even put my teeth in, I did manage to shove my wig on, even though it was somewhat skewiff!

Now for the serious stuff:
Water pipes are broken and all water must be boiled;
All buses are cancelled;
All public buildings are closed;
Hospital closed in readiness for emergencies;
All public concerts and performances cancelled;
All schools closed and in use as emergency refuge for people who can't stay in their own homes due to damage such as chimneys caved in, roofs off or fronts blown out;
All business offices and buildings in Christchurch central on standby until checked by engineers;
Engineers being flown in to help with the above although the airport is closed to general public.

All this is mainly because there are so many original buildings in Christchurch, built at the end of the nineteenth century. It is estimated that 500 buildings have been affected and could be demolished.

It might comfort you to know that all modern buildings in NZ (e.g. the hotels) are now built to withstand the quakes. However, several have been considered to be unsafe.

Blankets and tarpaulins are being flown in for homes that can still be used but whose occupants are in need of some sort of protection or comfort. Everyone is advised to avoid travel and stay home. To top it all, gale force winds are predicted! The rain comes down sideways due to the force of the normal winds, so it will be interesting to see what those are like!

Knowing that I have Jan just round the corner is something of a safety net to me, but it's pretty scary living alone when something like this happens.

Report no. three:

Due to the scientists' reports, we are all feeling somewhat overwhelmed. After studying the whole scenario, they pronounced that it must be 16,000 years since the last eruption of this magnitude in NZ – and guess what – I am here!

Our prime minister, John Keys, has now cancelled an appointment with the Queen due to the importance of what is happening at home. It has been announced that all the tallest buildings in Christchurch built at the end of the nineteenth century are to be demolished without exception. The schools that have been closed and made available for distressed families are so full that they have now opened the Addington Race Course (think Ascot!) as a sanctuary. I can only think that they are using the reception rooms since it would be a rollercoaster ride on the stands.

Water is now seriously needed. Thank God, I have a good supply of tonic and soda water – don't ask me why!

Even the broadcasting people have had to relocate. They have shown scenes recorded on the security cameras in supermarkets where the tins etc. have simply flown off the shelves while the shock tremors are occurring. The aftershocks that have so alarmed me tucked away here in little old Sumner have even been reported to have been felt as far away as Hawkes Bay in the North Island.

People seem to be moving around in a zombie state. I just had to go out for supplies, quite expecting a flurry of gossip with people comparing their experiences – but no! All were silent and really seemed to be in a shell-shocked state. Of course, that might be because none of us has had any sleep for five days now. How can we with all our worldly goods being chucked at us every few hours?

Report no. four:
Just had another night of it and no sleep. Once I'm awakened, I can't get back to sleep since I am so frightened. It seems more scary in the dark. There seems to be an exodus from Christchurch to friends and family living in areas unaffected. Lucky them. It has actually affected our family now, with Andrew's sister having to leave her badly damaged home with her husband and two little girls under five.

Although they live in a bungalow, their chimney smashed into the house causing severe damage to the roof. They were huddled under the beds at the time – which is what you are advised to do, to get under something solid for protection. They must have been petrified! Regarding my own property, I seem to have escaped any devastating damage, although I have noticed several cracks running down the walls, so I suppose I will have to have a builder round to check it out. Engineers and builders are coming in from all over NZ to help with the chaotic situation we all find ourselves in.

As for all my little knick-knacks around the place, some of them have snuffed it. I'm particularly sad to see my treasured collection of angels have flown away! They weren't expensive, but I really loved them. Ah well, Jan always did say I lived in a state of clutter everywhere.

One little story to tell you in order to illustrate just how forceful the tremors are is about the bookcase I have made as a sort of memorial to Colin. It is full of photographs of his life. The war years in the RAF, the visit to Buckingham Palace, holidays in Italy etc., etc. Well, as you might expect, loads of that fell to the floor but two actually flew across the room and landed on the coffee table.

The state of emergency has been extended another week, which means you can't go into town where all the unstable heritage properties are. They are saying that the cost of the damage could amount to $4 billion.

In her job, Jan goes round the farms and vineyards, doing their accounts. She visited a farm in the Port Hills yesterday and found that sadly several of the cows had been killed by flying boulders from the mountain and their little calves were wandering around crying for food. Since she is a keen rider, she always has a boot full of country-type gear – wellies, thick coats etc. so off came the elegant work clothes and on went the 'mucking out' gear. And there she was, running after and catching the calves, taking them back to a shed and feeding them with bottles of milk. She called her riding friend Sarah and, as they both love animals, they had a very satisfying time together.

She also contacted the local radio station to tell them about it all and they broadcasted it this morning. She was really pleased because it brings people's attention to the plight of the animals. A picture of her and a little calf was posted on the front of the local newspaper.

Report no. five:

Every day there is fresh news of devastation in the city. I really don't know how they are able to produce the papers, since the big press building was damaged and people evacuated.

Water is either unavailable or not fit to drink, so those supermarkets that are open have huge piles of the bottled variety. Some supermarkets are flattened, some are still standing, but so badly damaged that they are unsafe and some are open, but with very limited stock. I went out to my nearest one this morning and there was hardly anything there! I wanted some tinned tomatoes and there was only one tin left! It's so odd to walk along the aisles and see shelves that are completely bare.

It has been reported in the paper that the whole scenario has triggered a record rise in heart attack patients. Sadly a local church, just over the hill from me, has to be demolished. This really is tragic because it was built in 1858 by the very first settlers from England to arrive in Lyttelton. It was so quaint and special, but a huge crack had appeared right round the top of a beautiful stained glass window.

The cracks in the streets are incredibly wide. Some of the pictures in the paper are amazing and have shown men jumping over them in order to pass! Christchurch central remains out of bounds and the newspaper shows the police and army standing by in order to keep everything under control and discourage looters.

A jewellery shop just along the road from me suffered immense damage and a 10-tonne safe was reported to have moved across the room in which it was stored.

The airport has opened now and Air NZ have generously donated flights for Christchurch residents to escape further afield within NZ or even to Australia! I was tempted to ring and ask for a business class ticket to the UK but since I have discovered that NZ people have very little sense of humour, I thought better of it.

Jan feeding the calves has now been featured in the paper, together with a picture of her in action! She named one little lady Paris Hilton since she is turning out to be such high maintenance.

Something that was mentioned in the article and upset me rather was that the boulders that were dislodged and shot down the mountain (thus killing four cows) were the size of a car! It's bad enough to think of the poor animals, but what if it had been humans!

We continue to have on average three to four tremors and aftershocks during the day and the same during the night. I must confess that it is during the night that I really freak out. It all seems so much more frightening when it's dark. Only last night there was a great clatter and in the morning, I discovered another picture down. Needless to say, I am getting very little sleep.

The odd thing is that I have stopped worrying about the destruction in the house. In a way, I have come to accept everything flying all over the place – I just want it all to stop and start to feel calm again. Everyone admits to being in a stressed state, even the young. The place of work of one of Jan's friends was closed down. She was so stressed by it all and dreaded being indoors by herself, so she asked me if she could come and spend the day with me. I was delighted to have the company, but surprised to realise the extent of the fear that everyone is suffering from.

Ah well . . . there is no other option than to put on a brave face and hope and pray for the best.

Report no. six:

With the perpetual random aftershocks, all in the region of 4 to 5 on the Richter scale, I am really feeling very weary. We had nine last night and it's so stressful being on constant alert. There is a lot of posttraumatic stress, so all the hypnotherapists are working flat out.

Apart from the local newspaper, which is filled everyday with fresh stories and pictures of horror, we keep alert to the radio and TV for on updates. You have to admire people's nerve in making money at times like this! One of the local newspapers has even produced a Souvenir Earthquake Edition.

Actually, I bought one because it's not often that you experience anything like this! Apart from engineers and builders flying in to assist, the local demolition firms are overwhelmed with work. It is stressed that only real professionals should work in demolition since asbestos is a problem.

Food is becoming a slight issue. They have shown on TV the security films that are taken at all times, even when the stores are closed. It is amazing to see tins etc. simply flying off the shelves in empty supermarkets, really quite eerie and alarming to watch. The staff are working really hard to clear it up where possible so that they can open up for the general public. Shelves seem to be emptying quite quickly now. Good job I don't cook and can happily live on toasted sandwiches and jacket potatoes.

This will make you laugh. You know how commercial radio has those irritating advertisements in the middle of programmes? Well, the other day the broadcaster, in a very serious tone advised that, unless it was really necessary, we should stay at home. Directly after that, a jolly voice piped up; 'Dash down to Countdown. Their fantastic wine sale is now on.'

What was I to do?

Since Countdown is reasonably near to me, I felt I ought to force myself to go. Actually, the trip out was good since I hadn't ventured out for a week and it was interesting to see and hear how other people had fared.

The latest problem to rear its ugly head is landslides, which are causing roads to be closed. The train that runs from Christchurch to Picton is unable to operate at present due to boulders from the mountains falling on the line and since the road that runs along between the railway and the coast is also affected, there is no passage up to the tip of the South Island without a lengthy detour.

Although the cathedral was damaged, they opened up just a few roads so that people could get to a very heartfelt multi-denominational service held in Cathedral Square this Sunday, which attracted over 500 people. It was mentioned that twenty churches within the city had been badly damaged, many of them dating from 1865, when the first settlers started building.

I now have two cracks running down each side of my house. One good thing is that they have started a national insurance claim website!

Report no. seven:

It is exactly two weeks since the major earthquake and things do seem to be settling down. We only had two aftershocks last night, but they had a magnitude in the region of 5. Geologists and earthquake experts predict that up to and in the region of two weeks after the major shock, there is a 50% chance of having another 'big one'. An aftershock of 5 magnitude might produce its own aftershocks.

Although though we have reached the two-week stage, I think people in general are not finding it particularly easy to relax yet.

The damage suffered by Christchurch coincides with the seventieth anniversary of the Blitz. Considering I will be seventy next May, I feel I've copped it twice!

In addition to the heart problems and the trauma counselling, they have now opened 'drop-in' centres where people can go and talk about their experiences and hopefully get some comfort from each other.

We are beginning to hear in more detail about some of the injuries sustained. For example, as reported on TV, one gentleman landed up in intensive care after his chimney and roof fell in on him. He had injuries to his feet, legs, shoulder and jaw and he didn't look a pretty sight on the screen. I don't know whether I would have agreed to let the nation see me in that state! Sadly, over 500 pets have been reported missing – mainly cats.

Thankfully, Sir Edward Elgar is kept in at night and now he knows what to expect, he darts under the bed as soon as he feels the shakes!

I don't think he goes too far away during the day, because if I call him, he soon comes flying in. In any case, the garden is so big that he really doesn't need to go too far for exercise.

Now we have seen so much of the devastation in the city and surrounding areas, they have started showing us the damage to the farmland. The problem is that where the banks of rivers have been dislodged, extensive flooding has covered the fields, resulting in huge lakes where the animals usually graze.

Report no. eight:
I thought I was getting accustomed to the way things are but another huge surprise was to come. As this morning's newsreader said, 'We thought that things were settling down, but we had a real wake-up call last night!' I am left wondering when it will ever calm down.

Something I forget to mention in my descriptions of an earthquake experience is the fact that they are often accompanied with a terrifying 'booming' sound! Just to explain why one feels so nervous at a time like this, living on a knife edge and being faced with the unknown, here are the times and magnitudes of what we went through last night, starting at 6.55 p.m. and following through the night to this morning:

6.55 p.m. = 3.5 magnitude
8.30 p.m. = 4.0
10.42 p.m. = 4.4
11.23 p.m. = 3.5
3.14 a.m. = 4.5
4.35 a.m. = 4.3
5.04 a.m. = 3.4
7.27 a.m. = 3.5

Being so afraid to sleep but also so very tired, you start to doze and then find yourself absolutely shaken awake! And being alone, naturally, I am very alarmed. Sir Edward is no help to me.

Report no. nine:

Do you remember the song that Tom Jones used to sing about the 'Green, Green Grass of Home', full of reminiscing and longing? Well, in spite of all the beauty I have around me here, in truth, I have found it very hard to let go of my old life. During this traumatic experience, I have tried to keep the old British stiff upper lip going, but now I am feeling totally drained. The scenario I have been playing out is very similar to that in one of the old *Carry On* films. The one I have in mind is *Carry On Up the Khyber*.

It is during an elegant dinner party where the upper-class English twits, although being savagely attacked by the natives, show their stiff upper lip by continuing to enjoy their dinner with the string quartet gently playing, all the while simply ignoring the chandeliers that are swinging over their heads and the total devastation happening all around! Reading yesterday's record you will understand what I mean.

Yesterday (Thursday 16th) went like this:
3.13 a.m. = 4.5 magnitude

4.35 a.m. = 4.3
5.04 a.m. = 3.4
5.37 a.m. = 3.7
5.58 a.m. = 3.5
7.24 a.m. = 3.5
Evening and night:
5.53 p.m. = 4.2
7.35 p.m. = 3.7
10.36 p.m. = 4.1
10.56 p.m. = 4.4
11.09 p.m. = 3.4
11.23 p.m. = 3.1
Still in the night, but now Friday:
1.32 a.m. = 3.4

Reading that, I think it fair to admit to being overwhelmingly tired and afraid. In fact, I am rather concerned because my head seems to be swimming even when all is calm – I hope I'm not developing some sort of neurosis and I'm not joking when I say that. I felt most peculiar last night. I'm really feeling somewhat fragile and I just want it to all end.

Report no. ten:

I'm not even sure I should give you the latest update in case you might think I am imagining it or exaggerating it. The general weather forecast is for severe weather warnings, huge snow storms and gale force winds! Not in the Christchurch area but in other parts of the country – hurrah!

The West Coast has had waves 17 metres high! Further south from Christchurch, they have had terrific snowstorms which have caused roofs to fall in and crash power supplies. They say it is similar to the earthquake, only this time caused by winds. (What some people will do to 'keep up with the Joneses'!)

The North Island has had the same sort of problems with snow bringing about blocked motorways etc. As for us, heavy sea swells are causing car parks to be swallowed under water and park benches and rubbish bins to be swept away. They advise us to stay away from the beaches – hello? I live just a few streets away from the beach! I'm feeling very threatened by it all.

Yesterday we had seven aftershocks! And I was feeling quite dizzy all day, which rather bothered me since they had reported that the number of heart cases was increasing – possibly due to the fact that it was causing an adrenaline rush. (Oh, how I wish I had Colin here to explain to me how that works.) Anyway, I spent the whole day lolling on the bed and watching TV. About seven-ish, I decided to get undressed and actually get into bed to read. By eight, I knew I just had to go to sleep, so I settled down.

The next morning I awoke and felt altogether much better.

It was only when I heard the earthquake update that I got the most amazing shock. There had been seven aftershocks yesterday – three of them being during the night! And I hadn't known a thing about it.

Report no. eleven:

More devastation – not in the Christchurch area, but much further south. They have been having the most dreadful snow blizzards, even flattening a sports stadium. You may wonder why we have such extreme unstable weather conditions, e.g. this irritating business of having the four seasons in one day. I think it is explained by the fact that we are so near the Antarctic, which blows down icy wind even in summer. Also, because we are in the Pacific Ocean we have incredibly hot days, even in winter – think islanders in grass skirts under swaying palm trees. (If you ever watch any film set in Hawaii, look at the palm trees – they are always being blown around.)

Studying the world map, you can see that NZ only amounts to two dots just below Australia and considering that you can travel from the west coast to the east easily in a day, you will realise that we have very little to protect us from adverse conditions coming from any direction.

Something that really upsets me is that the Cathedral of the

Blessed Sacrament (Catholic of course), 150 years old, is to be closed for at least a year. This particularly saddens me because it is such a wonderful landmark, contributing a most imposing skyline to the area, almost reminiscent of Italian architecture (oh how I wish!).

Unfortunately all this damage to ancient churches and venues has upset all the plans for weddings this year. Usually busy from November to March, many churches and heritage buildings (for receptions) are closed for the season.

On a more cheery note, it is two weeks since the 'big one' and therefore we are just past the period the experts tell us about when explaining the pattern of earthquakes.

Yesterday, we only had four aftershocks and, thankfully, they were considerably milder than before, having a magnitude in the region of 3. Nevertheless they say that with an earthquake of such magnitude as 7.1, we are likely to have a few months of 'murmurs' as the earth settles down.

I think it fair to say that although utterly shell shocked, everyone seems to be coping quite well and getting back to normal. With the exception of the homeless, of course.

I must confess that these last few days I have been feeling strangely giddy, but I'm not going to bother the doctor yet and just let things calm down. Although I think I have been incredibly brave, I might be having some sort of delayed shock reaction. I do need some counselling. Am I right in hearing your advice to seek out some handsome young man, over six-feet tall and incredibly virile?

Now for some really good news. It will be the first day of spring here on Thursday 23rd September and in spite of everything, wonderful signs are appearing. Incredibly, gardens and hedges are covered in the most colourful exotic blossoms and Wordsworth would be overjoyed at all the 'dancing daffodils' abounding the roadside. (Actually, when I say 'dancing daffodils', I prefer to omit what is making them dance!)

Driving to the supermarket, I saw the most endearing sight . . . the beautiful, elegant, black swans waddling along beside the river with their little brood of seven cygnets walking between them. After everything else, it was a truly heartening sight – nature is still in action!

Report no. twelve:
Feeling slightly calmer a few days back when we had only four mild aftershocks, we were soon awakened from our false sense of security with a couple of big ones again, 4.1 and 4.6. Although not in the region of the really big one at 7.1, still very scary. The fact is there is no point in getting the house back to normal for a while yet, since each time we have a good shake-up like that, things start to fly again! I have been keeping all the newspaper reports together with the photographs taken by the press of all the devastation around the area.

Now for the really serious stuff. It has been reported that apart from our own scientists at the Institute of Geological and Nuclear Sciences, many scientists from Japan, the US and all around the world were arriving on the first available flights and fanning out across the country to do tests etc. Unfortunately, there is still a little uncertainty. Many theories have been published but the general opinion seems to be that the earthquake was a 'one-in-several-hundred-year event', meaning a once in 500 to 600-years event (I'm heaving a sigh of relief here ...). The experts have also said, 'However, the risks are still there, and the laws of probability cannot rule out another big quake tomorrow.'

I've just got to tell you – I am thoroughly fed up with all this! The aftershocks keep coming through, we don't know when or where and we don't know the magnitude until it is reported the next day. The front page of the local paper informed us that since the 'big one' of September 4th, on average we have been shaken every 29 minutes and 10 seconds, totalling 1,018 shocks! For example yesterday we had seven, of which three were nearing the magnitude of 5!

Report no. thirteen:
Well ... what an experience this is and certainly something I never, ever want to experience again! I have had several contacts

telling me that very little of all that has been going on here has been reported in England.

Facts: the earthquake in Haiti reached a magnitude of 7.0 on the Richter scale, NZ reached 7.1 (plus over a 1,000 aftershocks).

I think the reason that so much more has been made of Haiti is firstly because the earthquake struck during waking hours when people were out and about and more vulnerable, thus causing many deaths – whereas the NZ earthquake struck around 4.30 a.m. when most people were at home in bed. Which explains why there were no deaths in NZ as opposed to the colossal amount in Haiti.

Secondly, it could be due to the fact that countries like Haiti always seem to have so many people living in very poor conditions to start with, the media latch on to all the traumas of those poor souls whereas NZ being more civilized and affluent, the media seems to overlook the terrible things that have happened here and how the very lower income bracket have suffered. I wasn't aware of the poor conditions that some people live in, called 'state housing', the equivalent of UK council houses. On the TV, I have seen that many of these buildings look very colonial; pretty shiplap wooden cabin-type constructions. Of course, when the earthquake struck, these types of buildings just collapsed like houses made of cards.

These poor souls have absolutely nothing now. They tried to stay in what was left of their homes as long as possible but they had no water and no sanitation. Hundreds of portable loos were being trucked in, but even that couldn't really save them. Conditions were so bad that it wasn't too long before the authorities moved in and slapped notices on what remained of their doors, telling them that they had to vacate, leaving their homes and whatever possessions they had.

That caused pandemonium – most of these people have no money to up and move just like that.

I heard on the news yesterday that the hospital has been badly shaken, a very traumatic experience for the patients. It must have been so frightening to be unable to move from a bed with all that going on! Also they say that it will be months, possibly a year, before any repair work can be considered. The earth has much settling down to do before anything becomes stable enough again. The scenes pictured on the TV with these poor folk not knowing what to do or where to go were very upsetting to watch.

The dog pounds are completely bursting with all the pets that people can't take with them or rehouse and, as a little old lady, living all alone, I know only too well the comfort that a little furry creature can bring, how much you love them and how distressing it must be to part with them indefinitely.

Thank God I have kept every newspaper, containing all the accounts of devastation and deprivation since all this began. I did this because to me, it seemed such an amazing experience coming from little old cosy UK, and I thought the official record of it all would be of interest to any UK visitors I might have in the future. This will go down as part of NZ history, for sure.

I've listed a few of the things that I have found the most memorable:

1. Witnessing the major destruction of a city which contained so many truly old, elegant buildings and churches;

2. The very odd sight of the rugby/cricket field, just along the road from me, moving and rolling just like the waves of the sea and being left in furrows. That really was incredible and quite unbelievably eerie;

3. The sadness of pet owners whose loved ones have since been lost – mainly cats. Now I have my own dear little companion, I realise just how devastating that must be – I really can't bear to think of it;

4. That awful 'on edge' feeling, living in such uncertainty and dread of what's going to happen next;

5. Living alone – which I have had to adjust to, but it is terrifying when having to face the above, especially during the night. I feel I have coped quite well since Colin went, but there are times when I feel so incredibly alone, especially nights when I go to bed and say to Elgar, 'Do you know I haven't spoken to a real person today at all, only you? Thank you for being my

little companion.' Are you wondering when I'm going to be committed?

6. And finally, I have been so grateful for my sense of humour. It is wonderful to see the funny side of things. As the saying goes – if you didn't laugh, you'd cry! This made me hoot with laughter. In the local supermarket was a big sign saying 'Earthquake Special' and underneath a huge display of toilet rolls!

Report no. fourteen:

It's two months now since the big earthquake and every day we have new information to digest and think about.

They now estimate that, in addition to the 'big one', we have had well over 2,000 aftershocks. It's quite odd really because as I have been typing this, we have just had a severe shock which lasted under a minute but which I would estimate would be in the region of 5-ish and, although shaken, I find that I have quickly settled down to continue typing! Just goes to show how quickly one can get adjusted to circumstances. Odd, isn't it?

For those who like facts:

1. We have had over 2,000 aftershocks;
2. Approximately 50,000 properties have been severely damaged;
3. Approximately 1,500 properties are uninhabitable, leaving those people homeless;
4. Approximately 300 businesses have been so affected that they have closed down completely;
5. So far, 82,000 earthquake claims have been registered.

My friends Alfred and Barbara have been visiting and I was so pleased when they experienced a shock while shopping. I'm sure that one can never actually understand the feelings until you are in the midst of it and all around you is a convulsive shake, rattle and rolling. We were in a big warehouse shop at the time.

Apart from that, it has been so good to have someone in the house with me at night. In fact, I have had a good few nights' much-needed sound sleep while they have been here.

We went out and about, even to the theatre a couple of times, but there is an odd sort of feeling with everyone trying to act bravely and nonchalantly about the whole thing but at the same time giving out the feeling that they are ill at ease. The fact is we are all unsure when and where the demon will rear its ugly head and strike again.

The experts tell us that although they can't estimate an end to it all, they 'feel' we must be coming to the conclusion by now. I am so very grateful that the area in which I live has been affected in only a minor way compared to the centre of the city and areas further to the west and north.

Report no. fifteen:
We continue to have aftershocks but there is so much to consider:
1. We never know when and if they will come;
2. When they come, they vary in intensity, according to the length of time and depth;
3. All this, and we can't even be sure what to make of the expert opinions, although many learned people have flown in from all over the world.

For example, recently we had a shake out in the ocean and that put us all on tsunami alert. Apparently, the opening of the earth causes the sea to be sucked in and when it is regurgitated, it rushes back to shore causing havoc.

Only a few days ago everything had seemed to calm down, no shocks for a couple of days and then, out of the blue, twenty-five shocks starting just after midday and continuing well into the night. I didn't even notice since they were all low magnitude. So perhaps you can begin to understand the feeling of unrest and uncertainty that continues here.

I went into central Christchurch for the first time yesterday and, although I had seen pictures on the television, was shocked to see the devastation for myself. Many roads were cordoned off and demolition of the most unstable buildings was in progress. It really did look like a war zone!

After all the drama of the earthquake I am feeling utterly worn out, extremely tired and weary of trying to make a 'go of it' here. It is at times like this that you start to think hard and reassess your life.

Regardless of the earthquake, I have long been uncertain about my style of living since Colin went. I have put on a show of acceptance, have moved to the other side of the world and generally been brave, but I am beginning to wonder why. Without a doubt NZ is a most beautiful place and seems to have many of the best features of other countries in the world, e.g. Swiss Alps, Italian Lakes and much more. Yet it just doesn't register as such a wonderful place to actually live in.

Unfortunately, the two features I simply don't like are the most important to me – and they are the weather, four seasons in one day regardless of it being summer or winter – and the people – I have met some wonderful friends but on the whole the New Zealanders don't have the sense of humour of the British.

As for my home, I have everything that one could desire. I live in a beautiful house, surrounded by a large, elegant garden, situated in a quaint little village by the sea. All this, and yet I can't seem to feel truly relaxed or happy. I just seem to exist, trying to make the most of every day.

Perhaps that is how every widow feels when faced with the loss of her companion and living alone.

I must reiterate all this is nothing to do with safety and the earthquake that we have been going through, although I must confess it has been food for thought. It is to do with old issues that keep resurfacing in my mind. I just don't feel I belong. I have been considering returning home to England for quite some time now, but I am faced with yet another dilemma.

If I returned home, I would most like to settle in the Cotswolds, Colin's home area, where I have so many happy memories but I would most probably feel just as lonely there, away from the friends I have in Kent. Yet I am led to believe that the Medway towns are not a particularly good place to be. So what am I to do? I am totally confused. They say that England is finished, what with all the crime, but that's no different from here in NZ. We have all that here too and, quite frankly, I am horrified with all the drug taking here. They are so blasé about it and justify it as being perfectly normal. In short, I simply don't know what to do for the best.

26

The anniversary of the first big earthquake in Christchurch – 5th September 2011.

It is spring here now, the sky is blue and the sun is shining, the birds are singing and all the blossoms have persisted in flourishing, forcing forth new growth and imparting new hope for us all. Unfortunately the aftershocks keep rumbling on and we are all getting totally tired of it all. It can't go on forever – can it?

The situation is really quite interesting in that, after so many unexpected happenings, we just seem to calmly deal with the disturbances when they come. For example, I was on the computer the other day and a 4.6 rumbled by. It sounded like a big lorry going past and everything in the house, as usual, started to shake with things flying to the floor yet again. Yet I was in the middle of something interesting and couldn't be bothered with it all, so I simply remained where I was and carried on typing even though the screen was swaying. As it happens, it is a new replacement screen since the original was smashed during some prior shake-up.

We are all in agreement that we have experienced so much by now, we can almost sense the occasions when we can simply carry on with whatever we are doing or run like hell for cover. All very odd, and very tiring too.

For the last year, we seem to be just recovering from one incident when we are plunged straight into another. I think the uncertainty of it all is the worst thing ever. One has to get things in and around the house repaired as they are broken, but then you begin to wonder if it is worth the effort. For example, I am on my second set of wine glasses, the others having been broken even when nicely tucked away in a cupboard. The batteries are continually jumping out of the clocks. Doors can't close and I have had to get a gentleman in to readjust them. I have now given in and left all the books in piles on the floor since they have been flung off the shelves numerous times now. Photographs are now taken down since they have also been flying all over the place.

There are so many trivial shakes that it seems pointless in trying to get 'back on track' and most folk are living in conditions similar to camping.

Believe me, I am not complaining because the sights we see on television are far worse. Poor dear people have been without their homes since September last year and living wherever they can – in rented accommodation, with friends, in caravans and tents and even in the back of Jan's smelly old horse truck! Of course, the numbers have been swelling since the major February and June quakes have hit too. I am so very grateful my house is still standing even though I have lost a lot of treasured bits and pieces. Nevertheless, I still have most of my possessions around me.

I have a friend who lived in a very stylish property on the banks of the River Avon and was evacuated from her house at the time of the first quake on the 5th February last year. Due to the damage and uncertainty of how safe the place was, she was not allowed to enter the property until a few weeks back when she, like her neighbours, was told they could go into their homes for just two hours, just time enough to rescue any valuables. She was absolutely devastated by the experience. The first thing that struck her was the overbearingly awful smell. She then had to wade through the liquefaction that had arisen and being on a riverbank, you might imagine how awful it was. Mushrooms were growing out of her furniture, actually growing all over the place. It was all so shocking that she hurriedly gathered together important documents and jewellery and scuttled out leaving all other worldly goods behind. The whole place will be demolished and she will have lost absolutely everything.

In contrast, another friend who also lives on the banks of the Avon was only affected in one way. All her possessions were unharmed but when she took the house over, which was already huge, I might add, she had an extension built almost the same size. After the earthquake, the whole foundations fell away and when you go inside you have to step over the huge crack in the floor where you can actually see the earth below! All very frightening.

All this and yet yesterday, the actual anniversary day of the first earthquake, the people of the Christchurch area were remembering the date with celebrations! In the main square of the city, where the cathedral used to stand, folk gathered for a service and later in the evening, the whole sky was lit up with flares. Others gathered around the huge Hagley Park, linking arms together and on a signal all hugging each other.

As for the delightful little seaside suburb of Sumner, we had an afternoon of celebrations – one year on and still going strong. There was the usual bouncy castles, face painting, donkey rides etc. for the children and market stalls plus live music for the adults. I went with Jan and Andrew and a group of their friends and since the sun was shining and it was pleasantly warm, we had a good few hours, eventually ending up in the local pub.

Even after all that, it seemed so odd to be enjoying ourselves when all around the surrounding mountains one could clearly see the remains of those grand mansions, half hanging over the edge, contents strewn and smashed at the base.

27

My old and trusted Penguin English Dictionary tells me that the definition of 'metamorphose' is to transform, whilst 'metamorphosis' means a complete or remarkable change, transformation. I certainly feel I have experienced a sort of 'development' during these last seven years. When I left England I was what one might call a pillar of society. I had a career of my own as a teacher; I was married to a doctor, and was therefore expected to perform the usual duties of a doctor's wife. I also had vocal training which entitled me to be a member of Equity, and was therefore a professional in entertainment.

By the time I had reached sixty, both my husband and I had retired and yet I continued to indulge in entertainment by becoming an after-dinner speaker. Yes ... life was very interesting and full, but then came the event that changed absolutely everything for me. The death of my dear husband caused me to change my style of living and way of thinking completely, and emigrating to New Zealand just about sealed it. No more fancy clothes and enjoying the admiration of audiences but now the delight (ha ha!) of mucking out horse trucks and an appreciation of all things 'rural' and basic.

It hasn't always been an easy transformation but I think I have proved that it can be done. It's never too late to change and I am

A LEAP INTO THE UNKNOWN

thankful to claim I have been a 'has been' rather than a 'never was' – which consoles me. I am still here and I sincerely hope you have found some enjoyment in my journey and, maybe, some encouragement in facing whatever one might have to deal with in life.

In truth, I would never have thought of publishing my memoirs had it not been for the suggestions of my many friends. I have sent the monthly emails home, telling them of my escapades and, unknown to me, they have been passed around to friends of friends and even places of work where folk have actually asked, 'Have you got the latest report yet?' so I hope you too have enjoyed the tales of my adventures.

*

After seven years in NZ, I have decided to return to the country of my birth . . . Ye Merrie old England! I expect the first thing that might spring to your mind is the problem of the earthquakes and I am pleased and proud to tell you that all my daughter's younger set have great admiration for me, a sweet little old granny, and the way I have coped with it all. Nevertheless, after three major earthquakes and thousands of sizeable and very devastating ones, I see no option but to return home as the changes to my lifestyle and all that I love have affected me so severely.

Not wishing to appear as a rat escaping from a sinking ship, I must confirm that I was a 'war' baby, brought up alongside the River Thames in Gravesend (another elegant Edwardian town all those years ago). Gravesend was used as an obvious flight path for the Germans on their way to bomb London, and here I must digress for a moment and tell you of something that happened to my granny. She was in her garden one day as a German bomber flew over very low. Automatically, she looked up, and the young pilot who was probably no older than his early twenties, looked down. Instinctively, they waved in goodwill to each other, even though both knew he was on his way to perform his duty for his homeland. Every time I tell that story I am overwhelmed with the natural love we all have towards each other.

Anyway – back to the point I want to make. As a very little girl living in those times, I am thankful that I am made of stern enough stuff not to go scurrying home at the first sign of trouble.

I must say that I will be so very sad to leave this beautiful house and garden; nevertheless, even in 'normal' times, I have often felt alone here, and in spite of my many adventures, I have always missed England greatly. How could I not when I used to dress up as Britannia and sing all those great patriotic songs for any local, official functions? I've sat tight for eighteen months now, but what with Christchurch flattened and no remaining venues, all intellectual stimulation has come to a halt and there is little left to occupy me. This, of course, leaves me in the house day after day, lacking human company. Even the ladies that belonged to my 'Soiree' groups won't venture too far from home now, so I don't even have the delight of preparing entertainment for them. I have to face the uncertainty of driving out once a week to get groceries, as our two local supermarkets have been flattened, and, since you can never be sure which road is passable or which is blocked, or even if you are going to be caught in another devastating 'shake up', it is a relief to return to the sanctuary of my own house even though it means feeling isolated again.

I feel so very sad about the fate of Christchurch since it was such a grand and elegant Edwardian city but they say it will take ten years to rebuild and, at seventy, I feel I can't wait for that to happen ... so, land of my birth ... I am on my way home! And on that note, dear readers, I will wish you all the very best and send you my love.